Oh God, Why Can't I STOP?

HOW GOD'S RESPONSE TO FAILURE CONQUERS SHAME AND PAVES YOUR WAY TO VICTORY

JASON K. RITCHIE

HOUSTON, TEXAS

OH GOD, WHY CAN'T I STOP?
How God's Response to Failure
Conquers Shame and Paves Your Way to Victory

© 2022 Jason Ritchie
Published by Stellar Communications Houston

This book is protected under the copyright laws of the
United States of America. Any reproduction or other unauthorized
use of the material herein is prohibited without the
express written permission of the author.

The ideas and views expressed in this publication are those of the author and
do not necessarily reflect the policies or positions of organizations
with which he is affiliated. All content by the author is not intended to malign
any religion, group, club, organization, company, or individual.
The author's intent is to present ideas and views as stated in the Bible.

Some names have been changed to protect identities.

Scripture quotations are taken from the (NASB®) New American Standard Bible®
unless otherwise noted. Copyright © 1960, 1971, 1977, 1995 by The Lockman
Foundation. Used by permission. All rights reserved. www.lockman.org

Scripture quotations marked (CEV) are from the Contemporary English Version
Copyright © 1991, 1992, 1995 by American Bible Society, Used by Permission.

For information, contact:
Stellar Communications Houston
www.stellarwriter.com/jasonritchie
jason@stellarwriter.com

Hardcover ISBN: 978-1-944952-38-9
Paperback ISBN: 978-1-944952-37-2
E-book ISBN: 978-1-944952-39-6
Library of Congress Control Number: 2022904617

*To my wife, Ella,
who encouraged and served me
in every step of writing and publishing this study*

I waited patiently for the Lord;
And He inclined to me and heard my cry.
He brought me up out of the pit of destruction,
Out of the miry clay,
And He set my feet upon a rock,
Making my footsteps firm.
He put a new song in my mouth,
A song of praise to our God;
Many will see and fear
And will trust in the Lord.

Psalm 40:1–3

Contents

Acknowledgments ix
Are You Sick and Tired of Failing? xi

How God Responds to Failure 1

OH GOD, WHY CAN'T I STOP . . . ?

Falling into Depression 21
Hating 39
Judging Others 57
Holding On to Bitterness 75
Lusting 91
Giving In to Gluttony 111
Saying Things I Shouldn't 131
Being Prideful 145

A Letter to the Reader 167
About the Author 169

Acknowledgments

Many have had a hand in this project, and I share my gratitude to all of them for their wisdom, encouragement, and feedback.

God, for being my rock and refuge, showing me grace and mercy, and directing my heart and soul in the study of Your Word.

Jesus, for the sacrifice You made and for being so amazing, worthy of all glory, honor, and praise.

Holy Spirit, for convicting me in my failures and teaching me to stay in faith.

Mom and Dad, for believing in me and showing me the way. You're rooted in Christian values and have always cared about my future, both in this life and the one to come. You have shown me what an honest day of work looks like and have encouraged my abilities by promoting education. You've instructed me on how to handle money, how to save patiently, and how to spend cautiously. All the while, you have proclaimed that Christ is the way and to be wary of other paths. You've served as positive influences in standing strong against temptation.

Ella, for being my favorite person in this world. You are my complementary opposite and my compatible partner, a joyful miracle on earth.

Merritt and Emiline, for being my pride and joy and teaching me unconditional love.

Cole and Chase, for receiving me and teaching me new ways to love.

David, for introducing me to a walk that glorifies Christ.

My beta readers, for encouraging me to complete this manuscript and giving constructive and honest feedback on the material: Jeff, Gail, Danny, Russell, Karrie, Wes, Bond, Mauri, Matt, Helga, Liz, Chris, and Ryan.

Second Baptist Church of Houston, all the pastors, staff, and congregation, for investing in me as a sinner and a member of the body of Christ and giving me the opportunity to serve the Lord.

Are You Sick and Tired of Failing?

I'm referring to failing to do what is right when tempted by the sin of this world. Worse, I'm talking about failing to stand against temptation, against fear, and against faithlessness—even as a believer in Christ.

You are not alone. The apostle Paul was sick of failing too. He expressed his frustration in Romans 7:15: "For what I am doing, I do not understand; for I am not practicing what I would like to do, but I am doing the very thing I hate."

Our minds know the right things to do, yet our desires demand to be satisfied. And if we succumb, the failure laughs at us, mocks us, and says that we are not right with God.

In my own life, I have never felt so "not right" with God as during the failure of my marriage. It remains the darkest time of my life. I cried out in distress, "Oh God, why can't I stop failing? I can't seem to stop. Though I pray, though I study, though I return to You, I still sin, and I don't want to."

And in the aftermath of divorce, I wondered: "Will You still keep me? Will You still love me? Will You still use me?"

What does God say to these questions?

We have an opportunity to open the Bible and discover His answers. There are others who have failed ahead of you and me. Some of the greatest people in God's family have repeatedly failed. In this study, we'll learn God's fundamental response to failure and then observe eight ways in which many of us fail. Each chapter concludes with Reflection questions to consider by yourself or as a study group. Together, we'll find out how God responded in each situation.

It's not an exhaustive list, and you may be struggling with something not specifically addressed here. But God's response to failure applies to you and your situation. We'll find out what it means for you and me today.

How God Responds to Failure

THE FIRST TIME I watched someone crumble under the weight of failure was in high school. It was an unforgettable moment that involved a fellow senior named Tina. She was in several of my classes, including my favorite subject, calculus. Tina was a good student who tried hard to do well in all subjects, but math was not her strongest suit. Calculus was certainly not her favorite class. Every day was a struggle.

One day, the calculus teacher, Mrs. Dyson, was lecturing on a difficult concept when Tina's stress level hit the ceiling. She burst into tears, covered her face with her hands, and ran out of class sobbing, "I can't take it! I can't take it!" It was a classic case of senior-stress overload. To make matters worse, people teased her throughout the year for her outburst, including me.

Poor Tina. But as difficult as that day was for an eighteen-year-old, it seems to pale in comparison to some of our failures as adults. I didn't know it then, but my biggest failure would happen twenty years later when I would face the reality of a failed marriage. Unlike Tina, my failure came with adult-sized consequences that did more damage than a bad grade. And unlike Tina, my failure—and many of the failures of others around me—was caused by sin.

Since then, I've seen failures caused by all sorts of sins. Some fail in controlling their tempers or lusts. Some sin with their painful words.

Others sin in their bitterness or hopelessness. Still others cannot control their appetites for pleasure, wealth, and more and more stuff. The ways we fail may differ, but we have one thing in common: the private—and sometimes public—anguish of failure caused by sin.

Are you sick and tired of failing?

When I say "fail," I'm not talking about high school exams like Tina. I am referring to giving in to the temptations, fears, and faithlessness of this world and crumbling under the weight of sin. Even as we press forward in prayer and study, sometimes we continue in sin. Our failures mock us along the way, telling us that we are not right with God. We're left asking ourselves, "Will God forgive me? Will He still keep me, love me, and use me?"

God has answers for these questions. And, as we'll see in the case of Tina and Mrs. Dyson, God illustrates an amazing truth in His response to failure. But first, let's start by looking at God's response to failure in the Bible.

We can begin by looking at a man named Peter. It might have been surprising to some people that Peter was chosen to be one of the twelve apostles of Jesus. After all, Peter was a fisherman and lowly Galilean who was not regarded for his class or education. He was also a zealous, self-righteous, and proud man.

But Jesus knew what He was doing. As the Son of God, Jesus never sinned, and He never made mistakes. He prayed all night long when choosing the disciples who would change the world (Luke 6:12–16). He determined that Simon, whom He renamed Peter, was the right man to perform great deeds for God's kingdom.

So when Peter seemed to make a terrible blunder before the crucifixion of Jesus, we can make some interesting observations. As Peter's story unfolds, we'll see a pattern emerge that reveals much about failure.

A pattern emerges that reveals much about failure: initiation, progression, redemption, and retesting.

Let's take a look at John 13, where Jesus takes a final opportunity to teach His twelve disciples before His death. This is where Peter's story of failure begins.

THE INITIATION OF FAILURE

Peter's failure begins the night before Jesus dies. In John 13, we see Jesus pouring water into a basin and washing His disciples' dusty feet, an illustration of the servanthood with which His disciples should treat one another. After He dries their feet, Jesus explains the dreadful evening to come, after which Peter makes a boastful promise.

> [Jesus said,] "Little children, I am with you a little while longer. You will seek Me; and as I said to the Jews, now I also say to you, 'Where I am going, you cannot come.' A new commandment I give to you, that you love one another, even as I have loved you, that you also love one another. By this all men will know that you are My disciples, if you have love for one another." Simon Peter said to Him, "Lord, where are You going?" Jesus answered, "Where I go, you cannot follow Me now; but you will follow later." Peter said to Him, "Lord, why can I not follow You right now? I will lay down my life for You." Jesus answered, "Will you lay down your life for Me? Truly, truly, I say to you, a rooster will not crow until you deny Me three times." (John 13:33–38)

Peter is so interested in following Jesus blindly and without regard to the consequences. Now, I would like to give Peter some credit here. He is eager and loves the Lord. Jesus longs to have disciples like this today!

But though Peter is zealous, he is also ignoring the lesson from Jesus and being a little boastful on how sacrificial he is toward Jesus. I believe he is trying to prove that he is the best among these chosen men. In the version of this story found in Luke, the disciples are arguing with one another about who is the greatest among them (Luke 22:24). And then immediately afterward, Peter boasts that he will go to prison and even to death for Jesus (Luke 22:33). Oh, how we cannot tame the tongue! Peter is quick to say something that he really isn't ready to put into action.

THE FOOTHOLD OF PRIDE
Failure often begins when pride speaks boastful words:

"I know I would never lose faith in God."

"I am the most righteous among my friends, so I need to be the one who sets a good example."

"I can't believe this pastor is talking about lust again. I don't have a problem with that."

If we are so confident in ourselves when it comes to righteousness and blamelessness, I believe that God will put that confidence to the test. If we search our pasts, we may see that some of our failures were accompanied by boastful attitudes. We may have inadvertently brought on failure because we challenged it. God opposes the proud but gives grace to the humble.

In response to Peter's boastful promise, Jesus sharply lets him know that he is not ready for the impending persecution. Peter is quick to assume he is ready for the danger because he doesn't fully understand the grim things that are about to take place. What if Jesus had said clearly, "I am going to be crucified in less than twenty-four hours. Do you want to die in that way with me?" Peter might have sat back and realized that claiming he is ready to die is much different than actually being ready to die. Peter is not prepared in his mind or his heart, illustrating that ignorance can help lead to failure.

THE FOOTHOLD OF IGNORANCE

It was ignorance that caused a good friend of mine to stumble on a business trip many years ago. My friend drew attention from the locals as he was being escorted around town one evening by a cab driver. He was single and desired to stay sexually pure as he waited for his future wife. The driver did what he had likely done for many successful businessmen away from home: he took him to the red-light district. My friend was repeatedly approached by prostitutes and pimps. They begged him and threw themselves on him, telling emotional stories of desperation in hopes of convincing him to employ their services. He was far from home, away from anyone who would ever know what he would do that night. He was prepared to do the only thing that he could do to avoid sinning: he ran!

I hold my friend in high regard, and I am thankful he didn't fail that night. But ignorance led him to a place where he had little chance for success.

We see this time and time again when curious people enter the world of pornography and fail to its temptations, ignorant of its trappings. No one can be fully prepared for what awaits them in explicit movies and pictures, the purposes of which are to remove money from them as compulsively and habitually as possible. We are best served by never knowing what pornography offers, which means that parents should teach both their boys and their girls in their teenage years about its temptations.

When we are ignorant of the temptations that may come—in pornography or any other area—failure is very likely. Footholds like ignorance and pride come before a fall.

Footholds like ignorance and pride come before a fall.

THE PROGRESSION OF FAILURE

The stage is set for Peter's failure, but it doesn't happen right away. Peter fails progressively as the evening unfolds. He starts with pride and ignorance, two footholds for sin to work its way into Peter's heart, leading him to a test that he cannot fully comprehend.

THE FIRST FAILURE

We see Peter's first failure later that night in the garden of Gethsemane. Jesus is fully aware of the trial that lies before Him and takes the closest of His disciples with Him to pray (Matthew 26:37). He tells Peter, James, and John to watch and pray so that they won't be tempted. Jesus recognizes that the men have a willing spirit, but the human flesh can be so weak (Matthew 26:41).

Meanwhile, Jesus knows that He Himself will be sorely tempted to avoid the impending crucifixion. He falls on His face and prays that the cup of wrath will pass from Him, but He maintains that God's will be done through Him. Sweat drips from Jesus's forehead like blood as He suffers in emotional agony. He is preparing Himself through prayer so that He will not fail.

When He returns to Peter, what does Jesus find him doing? He is not praying. Peter, James, and John are sleeping. Now, I don't believe that they are sleeping because they are taking lightly what is about to happen. I believe that they are simply tired and needing rest, unaware that Jesus is about to be arrested, persecuted, and crucified. Despite Peter's big words, he is unprepared to carry out Jesus's simple instruction.

Like Peter, we may fail when we are simply exhausted. My mother used to say, "What is there to do out late at night except to get into trouble?" Indeed, nighttime is a period when some people indulge or do evil. I have found that I am sorely tempted when I am tired and my body hasn't the strength to fight. Temptation is a battle in the mind that wages against our bodies, and we give ourselves a better chance for victory by preparing our bodies through rest.

THE SECOND AND THIRD FAILURES

Peter had promised that he would stay with Jesus, which he does. After Jesus prays and is arrested, Peter follows from a distance as the rest of the disciples scatter. He sees Jesus imprisoned and condemned by the high priest, who casts false charges of blasphemy. Peter witnesses the horrific treatment of Jesus as the crowd begins to spit on Jesus, mocking, slapping, and punching the Son of Man.

The brutality toward Jesus reminds me of when I was introduced to the Ultimate Fighting Championship in college. At that time, in the early years of the sport, the street-brawl style of fighting required no boxing gloves and very few rules. Two fighters would trade punches in a cage until one gave up or was knocked out. They were so tough that they generally did not give up unless they were in a hold that would break a knee or choke them to death.

By the end of a particularly long fight, one man's face became so swollen that it looked inhuman. Knots that looked like golf balls under his skin covered his face, and blood was smeared across purple bruises. I never wished to watch that sport again. A year later when I came to know Jesus Christ and read the passage of the crowd punching Him repeatedly, I thought, "His face must have been swollen like that fighter. Yet Jesus didn't do any fighting."

I imagine that Peter has no desire to endure the fate that he watches Jesus endure. I also imagine that he is surprised when he is pointed out in the crowd.

> Now Peter was sitting outside in the courtyard, and a servant-girl came to him and said, "You too were with Jesus the Galilean." But he denied it before them all, saying, "I do not know what you are talking about." (Matthew 26:69–70)

Peter is unprepared when a girl calls him out as a friend of Jesus, a condemned man. Although he claimed that he would lay down his life for Jesus, Peter is not ready for the persecution that would follow. He denies Jesus as his leader, his Lord, his all in all.

Now that Peter is aware that he is in danger, he moves away from the crowd. Unfortunately, another confrontation awaits him.

> When he had gone out to the gateway, another servant-girl saw him and said to those who were there, "This man was with Jesus of Nazareth." And again he denied it with an oath, "I do not know the man." (Matthew 26:71–72)

Peter answers more vehemently this time, fearful of the consequences. He swears he knows nothing of this man named Jesus.

THE FOURTH FAILURE

Peter can't seem to escape unwanted recognition. The situation escalates when a group of people approaches him and accuses Peter again of being one of Jesus's followers. We see Peter's final angry response.

> A little later the bystanders came up and said to Peter, "Surely you too are one of them; for even the way you talk gives you away." Then he began to curse and swear, "I do not know the man!" And immediately a rooster crowed. And Peter remembered the word which Jesus had said, "Before a rooster crows, you will deny Me three times." And he went out and wept bitterly. (Matthew 26:73–75)

In his anger, Peter curses and swears that he is not with Jesus—not once, not twice, but now three times. And with each denial, he has become more hard-hearted. A moment later, a rooster crows, and Peter is reminded of Jesus's prediction earlier that night. What a depressing realization that Peter has disowned his God three times.

Even worse is the fact that Jesus observes this entire affair. Luke 22:61 reveals that there is eye contact between Jesus and Peter just as the rooster crows: "The Lord turned and looked at Peter." What a heartbreaking culmination of events. Peter goes from zealously following Jesus to zealously denying Him, all in His very presence. Do not underestimate the severity of Peter's failure. Jesus had warned His disciples that those who denied Him before men would be denied before God in heaven (Matthew 10:33).

Are we any different?

Like Peter, we fail progressively. It starts with a foothold for sin—perhaps pride, ignorance, or some other variety of sin that can work its way into our hearts. As events progress, the sin grows more and more until it is full grown. It hardens our hearts and does damage along the way. And when we fail, God sees it. What a sobering thought. A passage in James warns of this progression.

> But each one is tempted when he is carried away and enticed by his own lust. Then when lust has conceived, it gives birth to sin; and when sin is accomplished, it brings forth death. (James 1:14–15)

Being tempted is not a sin in and of itself. But when temptation is conceived, the progression begins. The path that begins in temptation leads to conception, then to birth, then to growth, and ends in death. *Any* sin can progress to this result. We tend to think of lust and greed as having the most tragic of consequences, but any vice can lead to death.

We fail progressively. Temptation leads to conception, then to birth, then to growth, and ends in death.

British writer and theologian C. S. Lewis made this point in one of my favorite books, *The Great Divorce*. It's a fictional compilation of encounters at the border of heaven with spirits struggling with a sin that is preventing their entry. In one encounter, a woman is constantly grumbling, much like the children of God after they were saved from slavery in Egypt. Her grumbling started small and innocently. I imagine that all of us are guilty of some level of grumbling in our lives. "The rent went up again!" "Our waiter is taking too long." "I despise the company's policies." I've said them all! Can small grumblings add up to complete failure?

C. S. Lewis explained that the spirit that had continuously grumbled ceased to be a grumbler and had become merely a grumble, having lost all personhood. In this case, the small sin of discontented grumbling progressively grew to the point of being full grown, leading to a spiritual death and no salvation in heaven. Although it's a fictional tale, Lewis bases his conclusion on a very real law of God: as it is written, "the wages of sin is death" (Romans 6:23).

Don't think that a small sin cannot progressively lead to complete failure. Don't think that it cannot happen to you.

A TRAGIC END

It happens to Peter's fellow disciple Judas, who betrays Jesus into the hands of those who would crucify Him. Judas appears to grieve the betrayal, but instead of repentance, he ends his life by hanging himself. Judas was a follower of Christ, even handpicked by Jesus to be a disciple. Yet he fails and has a tragic end.

We continue to see progressive failures today. One such tragedy happened to a man named Jihad Moukalled. Jihad was well respected among his peers, with a successful printing business grossing $5 million per year. He was fulfilling the American dream with a nice house in the suburbs of Detroit. He was a family man and had an attractive wife, three kids, and one on the way. But behind all of this success was a gambling habit that was hidden from everyone.

I'll be the first to say that playing cards is fun. And playing cards when money is at stake can be exhilarating. However, many people cannot handle gambling as entertainment. Jihad couldn't handle it.

There are casinos near Detroit, but Jihad took his gambling obsession to Atlantic City, Las Vegas, and even the Bahamas to avoid any appearances of impropriety. He would win some and then lose some—often tens of thousands of dollars. As the habit continued, the stack of maxed-out credit cards became three inches thick. He borrowed money from friends and family, then started stealing from his own business to fund his habit. Eventually, he and his family were around half a million dollars in debt. When a late-night effort to win it all back in Vegas ended in failure, Jihad flew back home and went to the office to write a letter at 2 a.m.

> *It is over. I can no longer keep going. Over ten years ago, I started gambling, and it has been as if time stood still since.*
>
> *There is nothing more destructive to life than gambling. I wonder why there are government agencies to fight drugs and not gambling. A drug addict destroys his life; a gambler destroys his life and the lives of those he cares about and who care about him.*
>
> *For everyone I owe money to, I have nothing to say but ask for your forgiveness. Family and friends, please forgive me. I never ever had a bad intent toward anyone. I tried, but I was gripped by the hope of "one more shot."*
>
> *I did not know how else to escape what I got myself into. All my friends have been helpful and generous, so were my relatives, but I guess I was beyond salvage.*
>
> *I have decided to take my life and the lives of my wife and kids. If they are still alive, that means I could not do it.*

I cannot bear the thought of what will happen to them after me. I did not equip them with any tools to go on by themselves, and I am leaving them with less than nothing.

May God forgive me.

Sadly, Jihad carried out the plan he had written in the letter. The authorities did not find him, his wife, or his kids alive when they arrived at his home.[1]

Be encouraged: for those who know Jesus, our failures need not end in tragedy.

Not all failure stories have to be this way. Certainly, this illustration is an extreme case that caused the complete ruin of a man and his family. I am not suggesting that all failures will end in similar catastrophes. However, we are arrogant if we think that our own sins that go unchecked and unchallenged cannot also complicate or possibly ruin our lives. A little "harmless" flirting from a married person in the workplace can progressively grow to adultery and complete destruction of a marriage. An attitude of "I deserve to pamper myself" can lead to runaway debt and personal bankruptcy. An indulgent appetite can result in heart disease. A hateful grudge can cause a person to despise an entire group of people.

But be encouraged: for those who know Jesus, our failures need not end in tragedy.

---

1. Casino City Times, "Gambler Kills Self and Family," November 22, 2000, https://www.casinocitytimes.com/news/article/gambler-kills-self-and-family-117919.

THE REDEMPTION FROM FAILURE

Amazingly, God proves that He forgives us our failures. He even forgives the predicted, repeated failures that must have felt unbearable to Peter.

Peter had claimed he would do anything for Jesus, yet he denied knowing Him in the face of persecution. Afterward, Peter weeps bitterly with the knowledge that he is not as prepared for his faith and future ministry as he had assumed. He flees in his grief.

Things turn around for Peter. Although Jesus was crucified, death could not contain Him. Jesus is raised from the dead by God, and after some time, He appears to Peter and other disciples while they are fishing. Peter jumps into the water in excitement and swims toward Jesus, who begins to cook breakfast for them on the shore. Imagine that: the King of kings, the Lord of lords, the risen Messiah, the Lamb of God takes time to cook a meal for His closest friends—even Peter, who had denied Him three times! But an even greater gift than breakfast is the conversation we see between them.

> So when they had finished breakfast, Jesus said to Simon Peter, "Simon, son of John, do you love Me more than these?" He said to Him, "Yes, Lord; You know that I love You." He said to him, "Tend My lambs." He said to him again a second time, "Simon, son of John, do you love Me?" He said to Him, "Yes, Lord; You know that I love You." He said to him, "Shepherd My sheep." He said to him the third time, "Simon, son of John, do you love Me?" Peter was grieved because He said to him the third time, "Do you love Me?" And he said to Him, "Lord, You know all things; You know that I love You." Jesus said to him, "Tend My sheep." (John 21:15–17)

Jesus treats Peter tenderly and restores their relationship. How wonderfully odd! This is Jesus's opportunity to remind Peter of his terrible failure. According to man's logic and reason, Peter has proven untrustworthy and should not be given more responsibility or authority until he proves himself. Instead, Jesus takes an unconventional approach. He gives Peter responsibility when he doesn't deserve it. He grants Peter the role of becoming the church's first leader.

The tender grace that is shown toward Peter and the prodigal son is for us too.

Jesus is full of amazing grace—and not just for Peter. Throughout the Bible, God restores His people when they don't deserve it. This is beautifully illustrated with the parable of the prodigal son. In Luke 15, the son demands his inheritance from his living father so that he can go and waste it on wild living. The father submits to the demand and allows the son to fail in his endeavors. After burning through his inheritance, the son eventually hits rock bottom and sees that he is worth less than the animals he is feeding. He returns to his father with humility and asks if he can simply be a servant in his house. The father refuses—not out of anger but out of joy! Rather than accept his son as a servant, the father restores him as his son. There is feasting and joy as the father celebrates his son returning home. He doesn't take one moment to condemn him for leaving in the first place.

The tender grace that is shown toward Peter and the prodigal son is for us too. Our God has high expectations of His people as we are tested through circumstances, and we often fail to show our true faith. But we have a God who always loves us, who doesn't even bother to remind us of our failures. In His great mercy, He forgives us without hesitation, drawing us back to Him and restoring us to our places. All the praise and glory and honor go to Jesus, who cleanses us from sin! Because of Him, we have the full confidence that failure is not a tragic end.

We are redeemed!

THE RETESTING OF FAILURE

It is wonderful that God forgives our failures and allows us to continue to be a member of His body. But this grace is not the end of the challenge. It simply allows us to start again and move forward as God continues to give us ministry and opportunities for obedience. We will face the test again another day, as will Peter.

Peter may have failed to live up to that boastful promise to follow Jesus through the darkest times, but Jesus knows that Peter will be tested again. He warns Peter that he will face persecution in the future.

> "Truly, truly, I say to you, when you were younger, you used to gird yourself and walk wherever you wished; but when you grow old, you will stretch out your hands and someone else will gird you, and bring you where you do not wish to go." Now this He said, signifying by what kind of death he would glorify God. And when He had spoken this, He said to him, "Follow Me!" (John 21:18-19)

Jesus prophesies that Peter will die in an undesirable way. We are not certain what that death is exactly, but there is good reason to believe that this is a description of a crucifixion. In fact, early church leaders believed that Peter was persecuted for his faith in Christ and was sentenced to death by crucifixion in Rome. Some say Peter requested to be hung upside down, believing that he was not worthy to die in the same way as his Lord.

It's interesting that Peter may have died in this way, but it is not particularly important. What is significant in this passage is that Jesus tells Peter that, anointed as the primary shepherd of the Christian movement, he will face the trial of persecution in the future. Jesus is warning Peter that he will be put to the test.

I'm touched that, yet again, Jesus doesn't bother reminding Peter that he previously failed Him in his test of persecution. In His grace and mercy, He remembers Peter's sin no more. Instead, He turns His attention to Peter's calling and his future challenge. Peter is forgiven, made the head shepherd, and warned that he will face the test of persecution again.

It seems that God, who works a process of sanctification and holiness through us, doesn't concern Himself with the failures of the past. He focuses on the successful outcomes of the future. God expects us to pass the test, no matter how often we have to face the challenge.

God expects us to pass the test, no matter how often we have to face the challenge.

Peter gets another chance to pass the test shortly after Jesus ascends into heaven when the high priest arrests Peter and the apostles and brings them before the Council for questioning. The apostles have been establishing the new church and preaching the good news of Jesus Christ throughout Jerusalem, which is dangerous since Jesus has been crucified. How does Peter do this next time around? We see his response in the book of Acts.

> When they had brought them, they stood them before the Council. The high priest questioned them, saying, "We gave you strict orders not to continue teaching in this name, and yet, you have filled Jerusalem with your teaching and intend to bring this man's blood upon us." But Peter and the apostles answered, "We must obey God rather than men." (Acts 5:27–29)

What an amazing turn for Peter, the zealous follower who denied Jesus three times during His most painful hours! This time, Peter does not deny his Lord and his God. Peter faces the oppressors and is willing to die for his faith.

Rather than kill Peter, the Council reasons that this movement will die out if it is not of God's doing, so the apostles are sent away after enduring flogging, abuse, and threats. But instead of being intimidated, the apostles rejoice for being considered worthy to suffer for the name of Jesus. God makes him retake the test, and Peter succeeds!

A PODIUM SWEEP

The retesting of Peter reminds me of Tina, my high school classmate who had the meltdown in calculus. In the face of failure, she gave up, crying, "I can't take it!" That would've been the end of the story, except for one factor: retesting by Mrs. Dyson.

Now, Mrs. Dyson enjoyed teaching this class and liked seeing students get good grades. In fact, I was skeptical of how good the grades were. Students received all kinds of special help in her class. Her standing rule about tests bothered me most: students could retake tests if they did not like their scores, and they could do so as many times as they wanted. I didn't think that was fair. Students could be unprepared for a test, get a terrible grade, and then retake the test knowing what was expected. And they could do so over and over until they were satisfied with their grades! The result was that almost everyone had an A average. We all appeared successful on report cards, but I doubted the legitimacy of it.

At the end of our senior year, our skills were put to the test. Our school was near Houston, and there was a regional math competition in which all the high school students would compete in areas of math. The competition categories were algebra, number science, trigonometry, geometry, and calculus. Several from our calculus class attended, including Tina.

We did not expect to win many ribbons. Two stronger high schools were there in critical mass, and as the results rolled in, these two schools dominated each category across the city. They won nearly every first-place ribbon as we waited for the results of calculus. Calculus was considered the highest level of math and was awarded last. Only the best of the best would be receiving ribbons, and our hopes of being recognized dwindled as the awards wore on.

Finally, it was time to announce the results for the category of calculus. After the tenth-and ninth-place declarations, the eighth-place winner was: Tina. *What?* We gaped at each other. Were they serious? We were still recovering when another name from our class was announced as the fifth-place winner—a student who wasn't even considered one of the top students in our class! And then another of us was announced in third place, another at second place, and another received the first-place trophy for a podium sweep by our class!

I was overcome with awe and humility. I learned something fundamental that day. No matter how much of a struggle it is to succeed, as long as we are willing to be tested over and over and over, we will eventually pass the test and succeed to the point of being stronger than anyone could have imagined. Failure is not the end. When we receive the grace offered freely by God, we are allowed an opportunity to try again until we have a successful outcome.

REFLECTION ON
FAILING

The Initiation of Failure
We can learn about the initiation of our own failures by observing the footholds that led to sin in Peter's life. His pride and ignorance set the stage for his failures. Are there areas in your life in which you feel a nagging conviction to address? What footholds are working their way into your heart?

The Progression of Failure
Failure comes in many ways. Jihad Moukalled is a devastating illustration of how repeated failures can result in a tragic end. How have you observed the progression of failure in your life?

The Redemption from Failure
Failure is redeemed by God's grace through saving faith in Jesus Christ, who died for me and you and even Peter, who denied Him three times. Instead of reminding us of our failures and making us feel guilty, Jesus wants a relationship with us and gives us work to do. Does Peter's redemption undermine the seriousness of failure? Are there areas of your life in which you need to release your grip on guilt so that you can cling to God's grace?

The Retesting of Failure
Despite his failures, Peter was tasked with a critical responsibility and warned that he would face persecution again. He passed the test. We're expected to eventually pass our test too. What test is awaiting you? Are there any opportunities to pass it today?

OH GOD, WHY CAN'T I STOP
Falling into Depression

WHEN MY DAUGHTER WAS three years old, she and I played a friendly game of Connect Four that didn't end well. The game was a little advanced for her at the time, but she caught on that it was similar to tic-tac-toe and that she needed to get four same-colored checkers in a row to win. To our delight, my daughter won the first round fair and square. She was so excited! She beamed in her success and was thrilled to beat her daddy in a game of skill and strategy.

We played a second round, and this time I won. I chalked it up to an opportunity for her to learn how to win and lose gracefully, but my daughter was anything but graceful. When she realized that she had lost the game, she burst into tears, complete with waterworks, wailing, and weeping. No amount of consolation helped. She was crushed and cried repeatedly, "I can't win! I can't win!"

What happened to the proud, beaming girl from less than five minutes ago? Any parent can attest to the fact that a child's demeanor changes as quickly as circumstances change. We've all seen children throw fits, especially when it's time to leave. And we've all chuckled about the terrible twos.

But the abrupt change of attitude based on circumstances doesn't only apply to children. Adults are also susceptible to suddenly falling into a depressed state—and then sometimes staying there. Perhaps the depression is triggered by a negative comment or negative life change. Regardless of the cause, chances are that you or someone close to you struggles with bouts of depression.

Are you crying out to God, "Why can't I stop being depressed?" How are friends and families supposed to deal with depressed loved ones? And how does God feel about one of His people who—rather than being joyful as part of His kingdom—falls easily into states of depression?

We can find answers to these questions in one of the greatest stories of the Old Testament. It is the story of Elijah, a prophet of God who became suddenly and deeply depressed, even after a dramatic victory. The Word reveals God's response to Elijah and provides timeless instruction on how we are to respond to loved ones who are depressed today.

FROM GLORY TO GLOOM

As we open the Bible to the story of Elijah in 1 Kings 18, we see that the northern kingdom of Israel is in a backslidden state. The land has been without rain for years, a punishment that was predicted by Elijah, which does not make King Ahab, the king of Israel, amicable toward the prophet. The word of the Lord eventually comes to Elijah and instructs him to visit King Ahab, after which God says the rains will come. But in the meeting, King Ahab blames the severe famine on Elijah and refuses to confess his disobedience to God. Elijah challenges King Ahab to a duel between the one true God and the king's false gods.

The people of Israel congregate at Mount Carmel, including the 850 prophets of the false gods Baal and Asherah. Elijah explains that the duel is a test of fire: the false prophets are to set up an altar with a sacrificial ox and call on their gods to send fire for a burnt offering, and then Elijah will do the same with his God.

The prophets agree and call upon their gods, "O Baal, answer us!" (1 Kings 18:26). They dance and make all kinds of sounds in their attempt to make fire appear miraculously. All day the people of Israel stand around, watching and waiting. Nothing happens.

Elijah taunts them: "Call out with a loud voice, since he is a god; undoubtedly he is attending to business, or is on the way, or is on a journey. Perhaps he is asleep, and will awaken" (1 Kings 18:27).

That evening is Elijah's turn. He gathers the Israelites to him and builds a dramatic altar in the same way a performer prepares a stage. He piles stones, wood, and the sacrificial ox, and then he instructs the people to pour gallons of water on the altar until its trench overflows. Not only is a wet altar more difficult to catch fire, but Elijah is risking precious water during a drought. If God doesn't answer the challenge, Elijah will certainly be mobbed.

Without babbling or delay, Elijah calls upon the Lord. He wants Israel to turn back to God and asks Him to perform this miracle for this sole purpose. Elijah is answered immediately with all the strength that can be expected of an almighty God. Fire falls from heaven, evaporates the water, and burns up the sacrifice—including the altar itself! The people fall on their faces, convinced that God is the one true God.

Elijah calls on the people to eliminate their false prophets. And after three long years of drought, he tells them to get ready for the rain. As the clouds darken and a heavy shower relieves the crowd, Elijah is so full of the power of God that he is even able to outrun the chariot in which King Ahab is returning to his home twenty miles away. Elijah must be on top of the world: God has been glorified, and the people are turning to the Lord. The false prophets have been eliminated, and the drought is over. God has used him as a crucial vessel to reach the people.

But Elijah's story takes a dreadful turn in the very next chapter. Back at home, King Ahab shares the drama of the day with his wife,

Jezebel. She is the number one fan of Baal and those now-extinct false prophets, and she reacts by sending a messenger to Elijah with a promise to take his life.

Ha! What kind of threat is that? Her gods have just been proven to be weak and nonexistent. Beyond that, Elijah has been the vessel of the almighty God, bringing down fire from heaven. There's no way that the powerful prophet would concern himself with the anger of a pagan worshiper who just lost a challenge. Right? Unfortunately, the reality reads differently.

> And he was afraid and arose and ran for his life and came to Beersheba, which belongs to Judah, and left his servant there. But he himself went a day's journey into the wilderness, and came and sat down under a juniper tree; and he requested for himself that he might die, and said, "It is enough; now, O Lord, take my life, for I am not better than my fathers." (1 Kings 19:3–4)

What happened? Just moments ago, Elijah had everything in the world to be excited about. Yet so quickly he feels defeated, deflated, and ready to give up his life. This is more than just a mood swing. This is not mere sadness, which is a perfectly normal response to many of the challenging events in life. This is depression. We can observe four elements in Elijah's story that contribute to his depression—four things that we may notice in our own lives or in the lives of others.

EXHAUSTION

Elijah had been in a tremendous, all-day spiritual battle in which he emerged victorious because of God's might. In his excitement and the Lord's strength, Elijah outran a horse-driven chariot for over twenty miles. But even in victory, the body can only take so much.

Elijah had hit his wall. He must have been physically, spiritually, and even emotionally exhausted, which provided a foothold for depression. Depression and exhaustion are so hand-in-hand that they can either be causes or symptoms. Not all people who become exhausted will become depressed, but if you are a person who tends to fall into depression, you may agree that you feel tired much of the time.

We live in a busy, hustle-bustle world. Becoming tired may seem inevitable, but we must find ways to prevent exhaustion to avoid allowing depression to establish a foothold in our physical bodies. One way to prevent exhaustion is to rest one day each week. God created the Sabbath day for man because He knew that people needed that day. Even God rested on the seventh day; certainly we need it too. We can be busy and work hard the other six days of the week to allow ourselves a Sabbath day of rest, on which we can do minimal chores, eat out instead of cooking, spend time outdoors, or chat with friends and family over coffee or tea.

Another way to fight exhaustion is a healthy diet. We learn later in the Bible that four young, godly men—Daniel, Shadrach, Meshach, and Abednego—became healthier and stronger than the other men in just ten days by resisting the food provided by the king and instead eating vegetables and drinking water. A healthy diet protects us from being physically drained, as does exercise. Jesus walked everywhere he went, as did most people of that time. People who walk, bike, or swim testify that they gain extra energy when they exercise and feel tired and worn down when they do not.

It's also helpful to look at our busy lives and consider cutting some things out. There are only 168 hours per week, so we cannot do everything. As hard as it may be, we can start by sacrificing entertainment. We often lose sleep to screen time. Consider charting out the week, prioritizing favorite activities and letting go of others that don't bring as much joy.

After entertainment, take a look at your career. Is your desire for money or power borrowing from your need for rest? It's not worth it. A study by Harvard psychologist Daniel Gilbert concluded that happiness is achieved at an annual salary as low as $40,000, the income at which basic necessities are met, and more money does not buy more happiness.[2] We serve our families and ourselves well when we evaluate our career goals and balance them with regular time to recharge.

OPPOSITION

Elijah is victorious: all of Israel is now turning back to the Lord. But when King Ahab's wife, Jezebel, issues a death threat against Elijah, we see that it takes just one person opposing him to send the powerful prophet of God into a suicidal depression.

Opposition may be the most significant cause of depression. Many who are depressed feel that the world is against them, and while it's rarely the case, it can *feel* true. There might be just one person who opposes us, but as we see with Elijah, all it takes is one person to push us into a state of depression.

We encounter oppositional people and situations in many areas of our lives. In Elijah's case, the opposition comes from a person of authority and power. When we are subject to an oppressive or oppositional employer, manager, or primary stakeholder, the world can seem to press us on all sides.

Another source of opposition is a painful relationship, especially when the one you admire and love says, "I'm leaving." Although divorce or rejection involves only one other person, the world around us seems to crumble under the opinion of that special person.

The mailbox can also become an opposing fixture when we are struggling financially. Financial opposition may be caused by situations out of our control, such as bills piling up after a layoff, or it may be self-imposed, caused by poor money-management skills or spending addictions.

Any one of these oppositional people or situations can cause us to feel overwhelmed and helpless. In all things, remember that "greater is He who is in you than he who is in the world" (1 John 4:4). Jesus died on the cross for our sins and was raised from the dead by

---

2. Daniel Gilbert, *Stumbling on Happiness* (New York: Vintage, 2007).

God. We are not alone or helpless, left for dead in our own sins. We have been given the Spirit of Christ to counsel, protect, guide, and convict us. Regardless of our feelings or circumstances, we remain victorious in Christ.

ISOLATION

When Elijah fled for his life from the death threat, he arrived in a town that was quite distant from his oppressor. But instead of feeling secure, he purposefully isolated himself. He left his servant in town while he continued a day's walk toward the desert. He didn't stop until he was all by himself.

Depression almost always causes us to shut ourselves from the rest of the world. Sometimes our exhaustion leaves us with no energy to interact or be agreeable with others, with no desire to hang out with happy people. It's easy to slip away to the quiet confines of ourselves. It is important to acknowledge this tendency and do something intentional to combat it. Many fall into depression after losing a job and being unemployed; if a new job doesn't open up right away, a good option is to volunteer at a nonprofit, which prevents isolation and improves résumés for the next job interview.

If we find ourselves in a lonely place, fellowship is a prayer away. In prayer, we can lament our situations, ask God for help, and pray for enemies. It's very important that we regularly attend church and small groups that bind us together with other people. The body of Christ can offer sensitivity and compassion while we extend forgiveness to those who don't understand. When depressed, isolation is rarely helpful, but fellowship is priceless.

Fellowship helped me endure the darkest days, weeks, and months following my separation and divorce. I had to stay strong and provide for my two daughters, whom I saw weekly. At first, I was isolated in my apartment on the days my daughters were not with me, spending too much time with lonely entertainment and away from friends who were concerned about my choices. Eventually, I forced myself to attend a singles Bible study, a somber indication of my new, unmarried reality. But it was within that fellowship of people that I rediscovered hope and grace and communion, and I found out later that many of them were having the same experience as me. These friendships have stood the test of time, and we still encourage each other day after day, "as long as it is still called 'Today'" (Hebrews 3:13).

SELF-CRITICISM

When he was exhausted, opposed, and isolated, Elijah spoke with God in a suicidal prayer. "Enough! Now, Lord, take my life, for I am no better than my fathers" (1 Kings 19:4).

Elijah's depression has resulted in an attitude of defeat and self-criticism. He has already forgotten the miraculous things God has done through him throughout his life. He had provided unending flour and oil that saved and sustained a widow from starvation (1 Kings 17:10–16). Elijah had resurrected the widow's son from death (1 Kings 17:17–24). And he had defeated the prophets of Baal on Mt. Carmel, returning Israel to the Lord (1 Kings 18:20–46). Despite these great things, Elijah wants to die because he just doesn't feel good enough.

Does this sound familiar? We have much to be thankful for and have accomplished much in our lives, yet when a depressed state firmly has hold of us, we can quickly forget everything. We forget who we are, what we've accomplished, and how many people love us. We reduce ourselves to nothing. "I am just a washed-up has-been." "I am a nobody." "I am not as good as everyone else." "I am a horrible parent." If you are saying these types of things about yourself, depression has manifested in self-criticism.

One of the obvious problems with self-criticism is the phrase "I am." When we are focused on ourselves, we close off the world and become self-centered, not in a boastful manner but in a destructive manner. Being depressed makes it difficult, if not impossible, to put others first. At this point, it becomes difficult to receive encouragement from others, such as, "You are a wonderful person;" "Your wife loves you even when your career struggles;" or "Your service to the

Lord does not go unnoticed." Depression can become so firmly rooted that positive words cannot get past the barriers of self.

If you are one who deals with depression, then these symptoms and causes probably sound familiar to you. You likely feel powerless and uncertain about what to do. And if you have a loved one who deals with depression, you probably see the exhaustion, opposition, isolation, and self-criticism. You likely feel just as powerless and uncertain in your responses, wavering from anger to discipline to sweet talk.

What are we to do? What does God do with depressed people?

FROM DESPAIR TO DELIVERANCE

God loves His people. The Bible tells us that "God so loved the world that He gave His only Son" (John 3:16) and that "God demonstrates his own love for us in this: while we were still sinners Christ died for us" (Romans 5:8). "See what great love the Father has lavished on us," says 1 John 3:1, "that we should be called children of God!" Throughout the Bible, we see that God is patient and kind, merciful and gracious. His love, however, is not the "sugar and spice and everything nice" kind of love. God is also just and holy, disciplining and correcting like a good father.

A person who despairs has lost hope in God, and losing hope has dreadful results. When there is no hope, there is no reason to endure and persevere and stand firm in faith. A wise quote from the classic novel *Anne of Green Gables* states that "to despair is to turn your back upon God." We are called to hope in God, as the psalmist writes:

> Why are you in despair, O my soul?
> And why are you disturbed within me?
> Hope in God, for I shall again praise Him,
> The help of my countenance and my God. (Psalm 43:5)

So how does He respond to His people when they are depressed? Is He patient and kind, or does He dole out discipline and correction? We can observe how God deals with depressed people by looking at how he handles Elijah.

PROVISION

The first thing we see is that God provides for Elijah's needs. Elijah has dealt with exhaustion, opposition, and isolation, and then he criticizes himself to the point of death. He has given up. God sends an angel to step in.

> He lay down and slept under a juniper tree; and behold, there was an angel touching him, and he said to him, "Arise, eat." Then he looked and behold, there was at his head a bread cake baked on hot stones, and a jar of water. So he ate and drank and lay down again. (1 Kings 19:5–6)

God provides for Elijah with the most basic of provisions: bread and water. Certainly this is no banquet, but for someone who is parched and spent, bread and water are the differences between life and death. When God sees His people in despair, it is amazing to me that God, though His patience may be tested, chooses to show mercy and takes steps to provide. In whatever trials we may face, regardless of the pressing needs that we have and despite our temporary lack of faith, God knows what we need and sees to it that we receive it. When we are depressed because of opposition, it's encouraging to know that our needs are met by the almighty God, who loves His children and cares for us.

Some may think that recovering from depression only requires faith and prayer or a positive attitude, and indeed, for many people these are sufficient. But also part of God's care is the fact that depression can be treated medically. There may be a stigma of using antidepressants to help manage the chemical imbalance that occurs in some cases of depression. But I believe that the Lord has blessed doctors and scientists with the ingenuity to discover how the human anatomy works, and they have learned that depression can be a medical condition that needs professional treatment. This is part of God's provision, and He is the Great Healer, Jehovah-Rapha. I encourage you to consider getting help from God, from pastors and counselors, and from doctors and medicines.

COMMUNION

Elijah has now been provided for, but it appears not to make much of a difference. He still lacks motivation. He still is exhausted, and in all likelihood, his attitude has not changed. Provision is not enough.

> The angel of the Lord came again a second time and touched him and said, "Arise, eat, because the journey is too great for you." So he arose and ate and drank, and went in the strength of that food forty days and forty nights to Horeb, the mountain of God. (1 Kings 19:7–8)

The Lord has provided for Elijah a second time, but this time, Elijah is given some direction regarding what he is to do next. He is no longer allowed to just lie down in the wilderness. The provision has purpose, which is not to resolve Elijah's depression but to give him strength to carry on with what God has in store for him. Elijah now has something to do: something that is physically taxing but not mentally or spiritually difficult.

It's interesting that Elijah goes to the mountain of God, Horeb, also known as Mount Sinai. This is the same mountain where Moses received the Ten Commandments and where God's presence was manifested in fire and smoke, striking fear into the people of Israel. In telling Elijah to go to His mountain, God's direction for Elijah is simple: "Come to me." God is our Father in heaven, and He loves His children. When His precious ones are in despair and depression, He wants to hold and love us. For that to happen, we must go to Him.

For a person of faith in depression, it can be most difficult to go to the Lord in song, prayer, Bible study, and Christian fellowship. Depression brings on feelings of unworthiness. And indeed our God is to be feared as the same God who was revealed on Mount Sinai. But we must put behind us our fears, our unworthy feelings, and our despair because God says, "Come to me." As we'll see with Elijah, God has something good in store for us.

CONVERSATION

The provision and communion given to Elijah do not heal the problem of his depression. They are two steps in the process of healing. Now that God has provided and Elijah has gone to Him, God begins to communicate with him.

> Then he [Elijah] came there to a cave and lodged there; and behold, the word of the Lord came to him, and He said to him, "What are you doing here, Elijah?" And he said, "I have been very zealous for the Lord, the God of hosts; for the sons of Israel have forsaken Your covenant, torn down Your altars and killed Your prophets with the sword. And I alone am left; and they seek my life, to take it away." (1 Kings 19:9–10)

Elijah seems to come clean here. His complaint is that he has done his best to serve God, yet opposition is still before him, and he is all alone. Elijah had not discussed this in prayer until now. He fled and traveled far from the danger, and only now does he talk about his problems.

When dealing with someone who is depressed, we must be patient and look for opportunities to talk. Conversation goes a long way in healing the wounds. It provides an opportunity for the depressed person to express exhaustion, opposition, isolation, and self-criticism.

But conversation is one of the most difficult things to initiate with depressed people. They tend to isolate themselves and avoid encouragement or chitchat. They often want to be left alone with their problems. And when they do talk, the self-criticism can be frustrating, threatening to bring everyone down. Approaching a depressed person requires acknowledging that the conversation will likely be negative. It takes mental preparation to listen.

This self-deprecating commentary can get out of hand, so you must be very careful. The story of Job's sufferings is a good lesson on what *not* to say to troubled souls. As told in the book of Job, he endures terrible misery, yet his "friends" come to tell him how he has sinned against God and what he should do to make amends. They don't seem to have much compassion on the righteous man who has lost everything. Please, do not seek to converse with depressed people with the intent of telling them of all the wrong things they are doing. Be a good listener; try to understand; don't oversimplify the person's difficulty; and certainly don't blame God for everything. The point of conversation is to get the *depressed person* talking, not you as the counselor.

If you are the person feeling depressed, you may not be immediately ready for conversation. But be careful not to continually push everyone away and hide from God. People may not always respond in helpful ways, but we see in Elijah's story that God's response may surprise you.

GENTLENESS

After Elijah spills his misery, God decides to reveal Himself in different ways.

> So He said, "Go forth and stand on the mountain before the Lord." And behold, the Lord was passing by! And a great and strong wind was rending the mountains and breaking in pieces the rocks before the Lord; but the Lord was not in the wind. And after the wind an earthquake, but the Lord was not in the earthquake. After the earthquake a fire, but the Lord was not in the fire; and after the fire a sound of a gentle blowing. (1 Kings 19:11–12)

The first three ways that God reveals Himself display his power. Tornadoes, earthquakes, and fires are at God's disposal in dealing with Elijah and his depression. But the Bible tells us that God was "not in" them. It is not in those things that God speaks to Elijah. It is the gentle breeze, a whisper, in which God deals with Elijah. How amazing that our God, full of power and wrath, chooses to deal with one of His people so quietly and gently.

How often do we treat people with this same gentleness? I cringe when I think of how I've dealt with depressed people who've crossed my path over the years. Please forgive me. God shows with Elijah how to treat His people when they are down. Lord, help me be more like You.

The three powerful acts of God remind me of the different ways in which we often react to depressed people. The tornado that crushes the rocks around Elijah is like the hasty phrases we dole out: "It's time to get over this;" "I think God is teaching you a lesson through this;" "Things happen for a reason." They sound something of wisdom or comfort, but they can feel like crushing blows to a depressed person. A real Louisville Slugger would feel better. This is not how to handle the depressed.

The earthquake is like shaking sense into the afflicted, trying to convince them that they shouldn't be depressed. "God loves you. How can you be sad?" "A Christian is to be full of joy. This is sin." "You need to repent and ask God for forgiveness." Responses like these are nearer to hate than love. They are full of condemnation with no wisdom and no heart. And they can drive the depressed even further into despair and withdrawal from God, their only salvation.

The fire that could have consumed Elijah is like the destructive things that are said in resignation, usually after several failed attempts to improve the situation. "I can't take your attitude anymore." "I'm leaving unless you get better." "I'm not putting up with this." We have a patient God who does not lose hope.

God's response is gentleness. This is the softness we see in Jesus when He saw a leper pleading for healing. It's the softness God had for the slaves in Egypt after they were in bondage for four hundred years. And it is the softness God shows here to Elijah, the great prophet who won a historic victory over false prophets but turned to despair the very next day. God's heart is soft with these people, a model of how we are to be with friends and family who can use a gentle whisper.

We are called to be gentle, even when we are enduring opposition and trial. We show one another love through patience, humility, and gentleness.

> The Lord's bond-servant must not be quarrelsome, but be kind to all, able to teach, patient when wronged, with gentleness correcting those who are in opposition, if perhaps God may grant them repentance leading to the knowledge of the truth. (2 Timothy 2:24-25)

> Therefore I, the prisoner of the Lord, implore you to walk in a manner worthy of the calling with which you have been called, with all humility and gentleness, with patience, showing tolerance for one another in love. (Ephesians 4:1-2)

If you are depressed, you can approach God. He will provide for you, commune with you, converse with you, and—most wonderful of all—be gentle with you. Do not fear drawing close to the throne when you feel like the least of the least, completely unworthy. Recognize God's love and lean on His mercy. God is a compassionate Father who will endure your depression and is mighty enough to conquer it. And if you know someone suffering through depression, learn to be like God in His gentleness. Show love, and resist judgment, impatience, and wrath.

Don't fear drawing close to the throne when you feel completely unworthy. Your compassionate Father will endure your depression.

FROM MERCY TO MISSION

Honestly, I wish that was the end of the story. I wish it was enough to simply say that God is gentle with us while in our depression and comforts us as His children. But God's work always has a purpose. His compassion brings joy and peace, but it also brings growth and fruit. See what is put before Elijah immediately after God speaks to him in a whisper.

> When Elijah heard it, he wrapped his face in his mantle and went out and stood in the entrance of the cave. And behold, a voice came to him and said, "What are you doing here, Elijah?" Then he said, "I have been very zealous for the Lord, the God of hosts; for the sons of Israel have forsaken Your covenant, torn down Your altars and killed Your prophets with the sword. And I alone am left; and they seek my life, to take it away." The Lord said to him, "Go, return on your way to the wilderness of Damascus, and when you have arrived, you shall anoint Hazael king over Aram; and Jehu, the son of Nimshi, you shall anoint king over Israel; and Elisha, the son of Shaphat of Abel-meholah, you shall anoint as prophet in your place." (1 Kings 19:13–16)

Elijah repeats his plea to God, but God redirects him with three missions. They are no small tasks: each mission will shape the future of Israel and the surrounding areas. Most notably, Elijah needs to return to Israel to anoint a new king to replace Ahab and his wicked wife, Jezebel.

God would not have us run away from our problems. It may be His will that we conquer whatever or whomever is opposing us. His way may be to destroy the very thing that causes our depression. Or He may tell us that His strength is perfected in our weakness, that we are to overcome our feelings to push forward in complete faith in Him. It is written, "His ways are not our ways" (Isaiah 55:8–9).

His solution may be radically unpredictable. He is an awesome and amazing God!

Elijah's next step is an incredible moment of faith. He departed. We know that Elijah still feels depressed, yet he is obedient to God's call. Despite his feelings, Elijah trusts God enough to get up and face another day. With God's help, Elijah musters the courage to put one foot in front of another. He conquers his depression through faith.

> For whatever is born of God overcomes the world; and this is the victory that has overcome the world—our faith. (1 John 5:4)

Know that God loves you. Know that He will not abandon you. God has seen His very best people struggle with the same problems we deal with today. He is no different today than He was in the ancient days of Elijah. God can save us. Let Him save you.

REFLECTION ON
FALLING INTO DEPRESSION

From Glory to Gloom
Elijah's victories become buried under his feelings of despair due to four factors: exhaustion, opposition, isolation, and self-criticism. If feelings of discouragement are threatening to overcome your progress, do you recognize any of these four factors in your life? What changes can you make to restore your view?

From Despair to Deliverance
Some of us may find God's response to Elijah unexpected—quite different from our expectations and reactions to depression in others and in ourselves. We see that Elijah does not pull himself together quickly. God offers provision, communion, conversation, and gentleness. How will you change the way you treat yourself and others who are depressed?

From Mercy to Mission
After God ministers to Elijah, He lets Elijah know that He has more work for him to do. Despite Elijah's feelings—despite the fact that he may not have yet overcome his depression—Elijah gets up and answers God's call. What mission lies before you? How can you exercise your faith in God today?

OH GOD, WHY CAN'T I STOP
Hating

HAVE YOU NOTICED THAT a person's name can trigger thoughts or feelings in your heart? Some names conjure feelings of love, friendship, or joy, while others draw irritation, hurt, or disappointment. Mother Teresa may bring thoughts of tenderness, while Adolf Hitler may bring thoughts of evil.

While most people would say that Adolf Hitler is the epitome of evil, it could be argued that Joseph Stalin was even worse. Stalin was a rebellious young man who fought against the Russian government to impose a Marxist regime. He was the protégé of Vladimir Lenin, an equally cold tyrant. To achieve his goals, Stalin murdered not only innocent Russians but also fellow Communists he perceived as rivals. His zeal for power and the mistreatment of peasants drove his second wife to suicide. He was a ruthless, insensitive man, seemingly without a soul.

Stalin's treachery became amplified as he grew more powerful in the Soviet Union. He presided over a strategy to purposely starve millions of people to death. Known as the Great Famine, this period was not caused by drought or locusts or natural disasters but by Stalin's policies to industrialize Ukraine. He turned farms into state-run enterprises and banished the peasant farmers to prisons, homelessness, or death. The images of those starving people are horrifying.

The Soviet Union was one of the great enemies of the church, killing an estimated twelve to twenty million people, mostly Orthodox Christians. Stalin implemented a scientific atheism and purged bishops and priests, forbid any form of worship, and burned down churches. Christians were sent to prisons and labor camps, not unlike the concentration camps of Nazi Germany. The evil only began to subside when Stalin needed to recruit soldiers for World War II and rally support from Christian nations around the world.

It is a sobering thought that such a despicable leader could rise to power in modern times and create so much death and suffering for his own people. He should have been brutally punished for the great evil he inflicted. Am I entitled to hatred toward a person like Stalin? Is it possible to feel any compassion for a man who has done such terrible things? Are we ever allowed to justly hate some people?

These questions become complicated when they're not about someone in another nation. What about the ill will we may secretly wish upon people in our own lives: an abusive parent, an ex-spouse, or a manipulative coworker? When someone in our lives has done us wrong, what sort of justice will pacify our loathing? Is there any way we can overcome strong feelings and find forgiveness?

We can turn to a powerful lesson in the Bible for some guidance. The story of Jonah helps us address the hatred we may hold in our hearts.

THE SIGN OF JONAH

Many of us have heard the first two chapters of the story of Jonah, the prophet whom God commanded to speak in Nineveh, a great city in Assyria, modern-day northern Iraq. You may remember that Jonah disobeyed God and sailed instead to Tarshish, likely a port town on the coast of modern-day Spain. If you know your geography, you'll recognize that these two cities couldn't be much farther apart—about 2,500 miles!

God sent a storm that tossed the boat violently and caused the sailors to fear for their lives. When Jonah confessed to the sailors that his God, Jehovah, was angry with him for disobeying, they threw him overboard at his own request. Jonah was apparently willing to die to save the others. Immediately the storm was calmed, and the sailors were saved. Even more awesome was Jonah's fate: he was swallowed up by a great fish and survived in its belly for three days. He prayed to God, and shortly after, Jonah was spat out onto land.

For many of us, Jonah's survival is the end of the story, one that shows a great miracle of God. However, there are still two more chapters in the book of Jonah, and they reveal God's convicting truth.

After saving Jonah from the fish, God again asks him to go to Nineveh. This time, Jonah obeys. He preaches a message of God's destruction: God will destroy Nineveh in forty days. The message causes fear and mourning in the city—so much wailing that word reaches the king, who also laments the coming wrath of God. He declares a forty-day fast in hopes that God will relent. Because of their humble response, God decides not to destroy the city as Jonah had warned. He displays His amazing mercy.

In fact, we discover much later—during Jesus's ministry—the full extent of God's mercy toward the Ninevites. When the Jewish religious leadership remained unconvinced that Jesus was the Messiah and demanded more proof, despite the many signs and miracles He performed, Jesus reminded them about the ancient story of Jonah and shared the ultimate fate of the Ninevites.

> Then some of the scribes and Pharisees said to Him, "Teacher, we want to see a sign from You." But He answered and said to them, "An evil and adulterous generation craves for a sign; and yet no sign will be given to it but the sign of Jonah the prophet; for just as Jonah was three days and three nights in the belly of the sea monster, so will the Son of Man be three days and three

nights in the heart of the earth. The men of Nineveh will stand up with this generation at the judgment, and will condemn it because they repented at the preaching of Jonah; and behold, something greater than Jonah is here." (Matthew 12:38–41)

Jesus referenced the story of Jonah to predict His own death and resurrection. The three days and nights that Jonah suffered in the sea monster is an allegorical story pointing to Jesus's death and burial. Like Jonah, Jesus would not be consumed forever. Jesus presents this truth as the ultimate sign of our Lord: anyone who believes in this sign—Jesus's death and resurrection—is a Christian and adopted into the family of God. Unfortunately, whereas the Ninevites repented at Jonah's message and were saved by God, the Israelites stand in contrast and refuse to repent. Jesus tells them that these same Ninevites from Jonah's time will one day judge the current generation in Israel.

What an amazing turn of events for Jonah and the Ninevites. Jonah first avoids the Ninevites, but when he eventually preaches to them, they repent. Have you experienced or witnessed an unlikely transformation of a person or group of people who have turned from wrongdoing and embraced godly living? It is possible in Christ. Not only are the Ninevites shown God's mercy, but Jesus elevates them to judge over the generation of Israelites of Jesus's time on earth.

You'd think that Jonah would be overwhelmed with joy to see an entire city repent and receive God's blessings. But Jonah was not happy. The final chapter of the book of Jonah reveals that he hated the Ninevites.

THE SELFISHNESS OF JONAH

The first chapter tells us that Jonah is instructed to go to Nineveh and that he disobeys. But it doesn't tell us why. Notice the lack of explanation in the Scripture.

> The word of the Lord came to Jonah the son of Amittai saying, "Arise, go to Nineveh the great city and cry against it, for their wickedness has come up before Me." But Jonah rose up to flee to Tarshish from the presence of the Lord. So he went down to Joppa, found a ship which was going to Tarshish, paid the fare and went down into it to go with them to Tarshish from the presence of the Lord. (Jonah 1:1-3)

Jonah eventually preaches in Nineveh, but not until he endures a tempest at sea, a three-day asylum in a great fish, and a second command to go to Nineveh. After preaching against Nineveh, the people repent of their deeds, and God shows mercy. But in the final chapter, Jonah reveals his true intentions for not initially going to Nineveh.

> But it greatly displeased Jonah and he became angry. He prayed to the Lord and said, "Please Lord, was not this what I said while I was still in my own country? Therefore in order to forestall this I fled to Tarshish, for I knew that You are a gracious and compassionate God, slow to anger and abundant in lovingkindness, and one who relents concerning calamity. Therefore now, O Lord, please take my life from me, for death is better to me than life." (Jonah 4:1-3)

Jonah's attitude is clear: he is upset that God would show compassion on the Ninevites and would rather die than see them redeemed. Does it surprise you that a prophet of God wants to see people destroyed even though they repent? It may help to understand the background of the Ninevites.

Nineveh was the capital city of the Assyrian Empire, an enemy of Israel. There are several passages in the Bible focused on prophecies against this city and the Assyrian Empire, particularly from the prophet Nahum. These prophecies were fulfilled in 612 BC at the hands of Babylon and other nations. At the height of the Assyrian reign, they ruled the Fertile Crescent and expanded through Israel and into Egypt. Thus, they were the world's most powerful nation, generally during the reign of Tiglath-pileser III, who ruled from 745 to 727 BC.

The Assyrian Empire was not a benevolent power. Captives were flayed alive, impaled, burned alive, and buried alive. Their skins decorated walls, and their heads constructed triumphal pyramids. Though these acts of torture were typical of all empires, Jonah lived at a time when Assyria treated its neighbors like this. And as a prophet, Jonah may have known that Assyria would one day be used by God to discipline the northern nation of Israel; Assyria conquered Samaria in 722 BC and assimilated the Israelites.

It's hard to say exactly why Jonah was so full of hatred toward the Ninevites, but I imagine that many of us would hate a group of people who committed some sort of atrocity toward our loved ones. Many films reflect our natural desire to avenge enemies who hurt our families. In the movie *The Patriot*, the character Benjamin Martin initially refuses to fight in the American Revolutionary War only to lead a powerful militia later after his fifteen-year-old son is shot in cold blood by a British colonel who had also sentenced his oldest son to die. Martin immediately begins a bloody rampage and kills twenty British redcoats, including a rage-induced bludgeoning with a hatchet. Sometimes hatred can seem justified, and Jonah certainly believes he is on the right side of the argument. He believes Nineveh deserves wrath and destruction rather than mercy.

As a prophet of God, Jonah knows God's mercy. Jonah hates the Ninevites so much that he wants them to have no chance to have access to that mercy. He is willing to blatantly disobey God—which is not typical of God's prophets—to deny Nineveh redemption. Jonah is even willing to die at the bottom of the ocean or in the belly of a whale before he gives Nineveh that one shot to repent and turn to the Lord. That is deep hatred.

Is it selfish of us to accept God's mercy and compassion and then deny it to someone else? If we have sinned and fallen short of

God's expectations and He gives us His awesome grace, are we in a position to think that we have access to grace and that someone else should not? It may be difficult for us to accept, but God said, "I will be gracious to whom I will be gracious, and will show compassion on whom I will show compassion" (Exodus 33:19; Romans 9:15). We are in no position, physically or metaphysically, to define the scope of God's mercy.

We are in no position to define the scope of God's mercy.

THE STUBBORNNESS OF JONAH

If you look closely at the transition from chapter one to chapter two, you'll see that Jonah was stubborn in his willingness to die rather than follow God's commands.

> And the Lord appointed a great fish to swallow Jonah, and Jonah was in the stomach of the fish three days and three nights. Then Jonah prayed to the Lord his God from the stomach of the fish. (Jonah 1:17–2:1)

The Scriptures indicate that Jonah was first in the belly of the whale for three days, and *then* he prayed to God. I can't imagine that Jonah was sitting in the whale doing nothing, but the text gives no indication that he prayed until he had suffered for seventy-two hours. This man has no desire to repent of his hatred for the Ninevites and accept the Lord's mercy shown to people who do not fear God nor know Him.

Jonah's prayer in chapter two is indicative of his stubbornness. Though we are not clued in on the reason for Jonah's avoidance until chapter four, we can see that the root cause of the problem was not addressed through Jonah's prayer. Jonah has directly disobeyed God's commands, but his prayer lacks any signs of repentance.

> I called out of my distress to the Lord, And He answered me. I cried for help from the depth of Sheol; You heard my voice. For You had cast me into the deep, into the heart of the seas, and the current engulfed me. All Your breakers and billows passed over me. So I said, "I have been expelled from Your sight. Nevertheless I will look again toward Your holy temple." Water encompassed me to the point of death. The great deep engulfed me, weeds were wrapped around my head. I descended to the roots of the mountains. The earth with its bars was around me forever, but You have brought up my life from the pit, O Lord my God. While I was fainting away, I remembered the Lord, and my prayer came to You, into Your holy temple. Those who regard vain idols forsake their faithfulness, but I will sacrifice to You with the voice of thanksgiving. That which I have vowed I will pay. Salvation is from the Lord. (Jonah 2:2–9)

This is a beautiful prayer that shows the source of our salvation: in the depths of our troubles, we are to look to God and have hope that He will hear us, remember us, revive us, and save us. But Jonah's prayer fails to address the basic fact that he ran away from God because he hated the Ninevites. In his stubbornness, he will remain unchanged from the suffering that God used to discipline him. That is why—after Jonah is spat from the whale—God has to command him *again* to preach to Nineveh.

> Now the word of the Lord came to Jonah the second time, saying, "Arise, go to Nineveh the great city and proclaim to it the proclamation which I am going to tell you." (Jonah 3:1–2)

Has God shown you to be stubbornly hateful toward someone in your life? Have you suffered pain and hurt and now find your heels dug in deep, clinging to a hatred that drives you from God? Perhaps yours is a deep resentment toward a group of people defined by a physical characteristic or philosophical belief—people for whom you refuse to acknowledge God's love.

THE SCHOOLING OF JONAH

God rarely asks men questions in the Bible, but now he asks Jonah a direct question.

> "Do you have a good reason to be angry?" (Jonah 4:4)

We see throughout the Bible that when God asks a question, it's followed by a painful lesson. For instance, when Job laments about his misfortune for days and challenges the justice of God, God asks in Job 38:4, "Where were you when I laid the foundations of the earth?" After that, Job receives a lesson in humility.

We also see this in the garden of Eden when God asks Adam in Genesis 3:11, "Have you eaten from the tree of which I commanded you not to eat?" God then provides three punishments and performs the first blood sacrifice to cover Adam and Eve's sins.

And we see this after Cain commits the first murder. In Genesis 4:9, God asks, "Where is Abel your brother?" Cain is cursed and sent into the wilderness as a wanderer. Now that God has asked a question of Jonah, we can expect Jonah to learn a lesson.

Jonah certainly feels justified in his anger. He lies down outside the city, watching for what he hopes will be the fantastic destruction of Nineveh. He expects and desires the fireworks of God's wrath to fall upon the enemies of Israel. He wishes for the utter destruction of these people, with no hope of mercy.

But God uses a peculiar illustration to show Jonah that he has no right to be angry about God's mercy. As Jonah waits, God provides a leafy plant that grows up over Jonah to provide him shade and comfort. Jonah is pleased, but the next day God changes the situation, and a pointed conversation follows.

> But God appointed a worm when dawn came the next day and it attacked the plant and it withered. When the sun came up God appointed a scorching east wind, and the sun beat down on Jonah's head so that he became faint and begged with all his soul to die, saying, "Death is better to me than life." Then God said to Jonah, "Do you have good reason to be angry about the plant?" And he said, "I have good reason to be angry, even to death." Then the Lord said, "You had compassion on the plant for which you did not work and which you did not cause to grow, which came up overnight and perished overnight. Should I not have compassion on Nineveh, the great city in which there are more than 120,000 persons who do not know the difference between their right and left hand, as well as many animals?" (Jonah 4:7–11)

It's interesting that God asks Jonah the same question about the vine that he had asked about Ninevites: "Do you have a right to be angry?" God is showing Jonah—and the rest of us—that He sees a much bigger picture; our hatred is rooted in our egocentric perspectives. When we hate someone or some group of people, we believe that our perspective should also be God's perspective.

Can we see the person through God's eyes? God's love, mercy, and compassion on that person may be for the greater good. That person may become a better father to his children, a better friend to her coworkers, or even a convert to Christianity who is saved to do great things for Christ.

God's love, mercy, and compassion on that person may be for the greater good.

The latter case played out in the early church. A few years after Jesus was crucified, died, and rose from the dead, a renowned young Jew named Saul was educated in the ways of strict Jewish tradition and law. He condemned the "Jesus movement" that began in Jerusalem as Jesus's disciples preached and converted many people. Saul hated these Christians and persecuted them to death. He was public enemy number one of Jesus and the church. I imagine that it would have been easy to hate Saul.

But God had compassion for Saul. Instead of punishing him for his evil actions, He appeared to Saul; it was a personal, one-on-one meeting between Saul and Jesus. Through this encounter, Saul became a believer in Christ! What a humble moment for Saul, who would call himself Paul for the rest of his life. And what a difficult moment for those who had lost loved ones because Saul had persecuted believers. Could you show compassion to a man who was responsible for the torture and death of your friends and family?

It's a good thing that God saw a bigger picture. God saw a zealous man in Saul, and He used him for His good. In fact, it was for the good of all the church. Through Paul, the church grew into Europe, and many non-Jews were introduced to Jesus through him. He became the apostle to the Gentiles, or non-Jews, and changed history forever. Europe eventually embraced Christianity, and Western civilization grew from Judeo-Christian morals and principles, an effect seen even two thousand years later. All of this because God had compassion on one person who certainly deserved none.

When we look again at Jonah, we see a man who has compassion for a plant that he didn't work for, that he didn't toil over, and that he saw live and die within a day. But he is unwilling to show concern for thousands of people—and their animals—who have not had the same blessings as he has. Think about Jonah's very favored life with God: he is a prophet, a very select person whom God chooses and sanctifies. He was born into that family of chosen people, and he has received a blessing for all time thanks to God's purpose in election and through his ancestor Abraham's earlier faith in God. Jonah did not work for this familial blessing, nor did he have anything to do with Abraham's faith or trials. Jonah simply reaps the benefits of being a Hebrew and a prophet.

The Ninevites, on the other hand, have never had these blessings and have not known God. And in this one moment, the Ninevites are reaching out to God and praying for His mercy. Isn't it only right that God extends to another person or group the blessings that Jonah and his family have received?

Much of the good we see is because God had compassion on one person who certainly deserved none.

This is where I am truly convicted. I have lived a sheltered and privileged life. I was born in America, which automatically grants me citizenship in the most powerful and economically blessed country in the world. I have rights that millions of people throughout the world could only dream of having. I was born to parents who loved me and took an interest in my upbringing. I've never suffered; I've always had food, clothing, and shelter. I have access to justice, safety, and hope for a bright future. I've received blessings that have nothing to do with my efforts or struggles. Should I not wish those same blessings on anyone else who hasn't been as fortunate as me?

At the end of the book of Jonah, God spells out the reasons for His compassion. He tells Jonah that He shows compassion to the Ninevites because of the size of the city and the people's relative ignorance.

Whereas Jonah has the benefits of being born into a society that knows God, the Ninevites have known nothing of God's righteousness, holiness, and mercy. It is fitting that God would have a desire to show His attributes to such a large and influential city. He even shows compassion for the animals. God infers that if Jonah won't show compassion for the people, he should at least care about the animals!

In the same way, even if we feel justified in despising someone in our lives or a group of people from afar, we must realize that they are loved by God and that He would want them to repent of their sins and live for Him. Even if it never happens, shouldn't we have that hope for them? How much better it would be for them to know God and be known by God in the same way we do—to feel the same love, the same lifted burdens, the same joy? This is God's wisdom: hatred stirs up strife, but love covers all transgressions (Proverbs 10:12).

I haven't experienced personal trauma like that of Jonah, but there are people who have. Some of them stew in their hatred for a lifetime and never heal spiritually and emotionally. But I am inspired by people who testify of the power of God through Jesus Christ about forgiveness and compassion when they would otherwise be driven by hate. One such story is from Kim Phuc, an innocent victim of the Vietnam War.

Kim was nine years old in 1972 when her life changed forever from a napalm attack on a pagoda where she and her family were taking refuge. She suffered burns on sixty-five percent of her body, and she was famously photographed as she ran down a road in South Vietnam, crying and naked. The photo would become an iconic image of the suffering and injustice of the war and would win Nick Ut a Pulitzer Prize. It is a worthy recognition; the image stirs strong emotions in anyone who sees it. Some feel grief. Some feel compassion. Some feel anger and hatred.

Kim would struggle for many years through her trauma. She would have been justified in hating the United States military for the bombing of her home and the devastation to her health and well-being. She could have hated all Americans for the violence of the war. She was used by her country as a symbol, which caused her to be taken out of school and lose her dream of becoming a doctor. She admitted to hating healthy people because she was burned and traumatized, while others were not.

Kim said in a radio interview: "The anger inside me was like a hatred as high as a mountain. I hated my life. I hated all people who were normal because I was not normal. I really wanted to die many times."³

Though tragic, the hatred seems justified. She had so many reasons to hate. But Kim was drawn to God. In 1982, she accepted Jesus as her personal Savior.

"It was an amazing turning point in my life," she said in the interview. "God helped me to learn to forgive—the most difficult of all lessons. It didn't happen in a day, and it wasn't easy. But I finally got it."

She learned the power of forgiveness; the same forgiveness that God gave to the Ninevites filled her heart. She turned from her hate. She admits to still having physical pain and visible scars, but her heart is cleansed.

Kim now runs Kim Foundation International, which aids children who are war victims. She also started Restoring Heroes, which advocates for first responders and members of the military who have suffered trauma. She has compassion for those who have had similar experiences as herself.

"Living with hate and bitterness almost killed me many times," she said. "When I learned to forgive all those who caused my suffering, that was like heaven on earth for me."⁴

Praise God for how He works in our hearts to embrace forgiveness and to forsake hating.

STOP HATING

You may not have a dramatic story of injustice like Kim Phuc, motivating you to hate an entire world of people. But if you're honest

---

3. Kim Phuc, "The Long Road to Forgiveness," as heard on *All Things Considered*, NPR, June 30, 2008, https://www.npr.org/templates/story/story.php?storyId=91964687.

4. Reuters, "Vietnamese Girl Burned by Napalm Focuses on Forgiveness," *Voice of America*, March 22, 2016, https://www.voanews.com/a/vietnamese-girl-burned-by-napalm-focuses-on-forgiveness-in-helping-us-military/3249164.html.

with yourself, you may realize that there are other individuals or groups you secretly hope will fail. You might admit that you feel justified in your thinking that they don't deserve God's blessings, much like Jonah thought about the Ninevites. But John describes our justified hatred as walking in darkness:

> The one who loves his brother abides in the Light and there is no cause for stumbling in him. But the one who hates his brother is in the darkness and walks in the darkness, and does not know where he is going because the darkness has blinded his eyes. (1 John 2:10–11)

God commands us out of darkness and hate into His high standard of love. In His Sermon on the Mount, Jesus convicted His people with the truth about love and hate:

> You have heard that it was said, "You shall love your neighbor and hate your enemy." But I say to you, love your enemies and pray for those who persecute you, so that you may be sons of your Father who is in heaven; for He causes His sun to rise on the evil and the good, and sends rain on the righteous and the unrighteous. For if you love those who love you, what reward do you have? Do not even the tax collectors do the same? If you greet only your brothers, what more are you doing than others? Do not even the Gentiles do the same? Therefore you are to be perfect, as your heavenly Father is perfect. (Matthew 5:43–48)

Long ago, these words from Jesus pierced my heart and changed me forever. I used to think that I didn't have enemies, but I became honest with myself and acknowledged that there are people I'd rather not have in my life, people that I would wish God not to bless. I was like Jonah. But Jesus was calling me to pray for my enemies—not prayers of doom, but prayers of blessing and prayers for their prosperity. And yes, Jesus was teaching me to pray for their salvation.

Since then, I have put into practice the power of prayer to change my hatred and loathing to love and compassion. I've designated a day of the week as a reminder to myself to pray for my "enemies." My enemies are more like my adversaries, people who have caused trouble in my career or who have hurt my loved ones. Quite honestly, it's not fun: as I've prayed for people over the years, I've often found myself becoming grumpy praying for that person, dwelling on the wrongs done, and pleading to God to make things right. But God reminds me to continue to bless them, to hope for them, and to love them.

Amazingly, He has answered those prayers to my benefit. My heart toward my enemies changes, and I empathize with them more after prayer—even if it takes years. And every single enemy for whom I have prayed persistently has moved on to better things in their lives. They've stopped being adversaries to me. I stopped being surprised by this long ago: God calls us to stop hating and start praying because He is faithful to answer our persistent prayers.

Thankfully, God's thoughts and ways are higher than ours—as the heavens are higher than the earth (Isaiah 55:8-9). We have a great God who shows compassion on sinners through the body of Christ and leads us all to repentance. To quote a good friend of mine, "When we hate, we don't allow room for forgiveness." May He change our hearts, replacing our hate with a desire to show compassion for all people.

REFLECTION ON
HATING

The Sign of Jonah
After Jonah spends three days and nights in the belly of a whale, he obeys God's command, resulting in an amazing turnaround for the Ninevites. The violent people not only repent and receive God's mercy, but they are elevated to judge the souls of the people of Israel. Jesus used this story of Jonah to predict His own death, burial, and resurrection, the ultimate sign of our Lord. Do you accept Jesus's death and resurrection as truth?

The Selfishness of Jonah
Jonah does not want the Ninevites to receive God's mercy. Although he is a prophet of God, he is still a sinner who falls short of the glory of God. Have you admitted to holding hate in your heart for certain individuals or groups of people?

The Stubbornness of Jonah
Jonah goes to great lengths to avoid God's calling to preach to the Ninevites, a group of people Jonah hates. He runs away from God, putting others and himself in danger before finally praying to God and obeying God's command. To what lengths have you gone to resist God's command to show care for someone you hate? What impact has your refusal had on yourself and others?

The Schooling of Jonah

Jonah loses sight of the free blessings that he has received from God that are not of his doing. He has been born into God's family and has known God intimately, two immense blessings that the Ninevites had not received. What privileges have you received that are not of your doing?

Stop Hating

Jesus calls us to love our enemies and pray for those who persecute us. Do you encounter adversarial people in your life? What practical way can you remember to pray for your enemies?

OH GOD, WHY CAN'T I STOP
Judging Others

AMERICAN POLITICIANS ARE NOTORIOUS for flip-flopping on critical issues, typically saying whatever is needed to get votes in a hotly contested campaign. But occasionally a politician sticks to the same principles for a lifetime even when those principles are controversial and sinful. In one case, that political life began in 1933 in the person of Strom Thurmond, who ran as a segregationist in the 1948 United States presidential campaign.

Though unsuccessful as a presidential candidate, Thurmond became a powerful influence on domestic policy as a United States senator from 1954 to 2003. Thurmond fought consistently against civil rights laws, once debating for over twenty-four hours to set a filibuster record in the Senate in 1957. He remained unchanged in his opinions throughout his career, continuing to fight against civil rights in the 1960s. He never renounced his position as a segregationist, even though his unapologetic views caused issues within his party.

Though Thurmond's stance on race was backward and opposed to God's love of all people—and though I despise his racism—he still managed to gain respect among his political peers and was considered to be a man of principle. But all of that respect was erased with one discovery of a dark secret that had been hidden for nearly eighty years: Strom Thurmond fathered a woman named Essie Mae Washington-Williams when he was twenty-two years old and when the mother was sixteen. The reason this was a secret was not that the mother, Carrie Butler, was so young but because she was black. The man who spent a lifetime railing in support of segregation had been involved in an interracial relationship.

After Thurmond's death, it was revealed that he had a daughter who had kept his secret for her entire life. Details of Thurmond's financial support for Essie Mae show at least some compassion for his daughter and her mother, but all of his segregationist views can be seen as hypocritical. Thurmond's death revealed his shame.

Nobody likes a hypocrite who preaches against and judges one thing only to be found guilty of the same thing. We are rightfully angry when we see our elected officials, law enforcement officers, and judges fail to obey the very laws that they create and uphold. These men and women lose all respect when they speak boldly or walk powerfully in their positions and simultaneously break the law or abuse their power.

Are we any different? Have you ever pointed a judgmental finger at someone and stated that their actions were wrong only to realize deep down that you're guilty of the same things? The simple correction to this problem is to stop judging people. It's so much easier said than done. Let's learn from Jesus on this matter and look at the devastating consequences of judging from David, a man after God's own heart.

JUDGE NOT

The best sermon ever preached has to be Jesus's Sermon on the Mount, which is recorded in Matthew 5–7. It's only a fifteen-minute read, and it's worth rereading at least once a year. This sermon is delivered with grace and compassion that draws followers of Christ to repentance. One of the critical lessons involves judging others.

Do not judge so that you will not be judged. For in the way you judge, you will be judged; and by your standard of measure, it will be measured to you. Why do you look at the speck that is in your brother's eye, but do not notice the log that is in your own eye? Or how can you say to your brother, "Let me take the speck out of your eye," and behold, the log is in your own eye? You hypocrite, first take the log out of your own eye, and then you will see clearly to take the speck out of your brother's eye. (Matthew 7:1–5)

This begins with a simple command: do not judge. The reason? So you won't be judged. To put it another way, when you judge others, be prepared to be judged in the same way.

Personally, I have enough issues in my own life and my walk with the Lord that I don't have much right to look into other people's lives and judge them for their wrongdoings. I'd likely find myself guilty of the same things. I know, for example, God's Word regarding divorce. He hates divorce and only provides for it because of the hardness of men's hearts. A marriage that dissolves is somewhere and somehow rooted in sin, in most cases by both parties. But if I, a divorcé myself, judge and condemn a man for divorcing his wife, withholding mercy and compassion from him, then I would be a hypocrite, and God would judge me in the same harsh way. And if God withholds mercy from me, what hope can I possibly have? I would be guilty of my own judgmental standard and face whatever punishment God deems appropriate. Judging others is a path to my own destruction.

---

*If God withholds mercy from me,
what hope can I possibly have?*

I was greatly humbled several years ago due to this very thing. I was in my church lobby one morning when I ran into a married couple. I recognized them as one of several couples who had been in a married Bible study class with me years earlier. Back then, I had been a young man married to my first wife, and I had thought pretty highly of us as a couple. I recall having conversations with my wife about other couples on the way home from church, particularly about that couple. I had judged their marriage as insecure and at risk. Yet there I stood, fifteen years later, a divorced man. It was *my* marriage that had been insecure and at risk. They were happily married, serving in youth group and considering full-time ministry work. They were shocked when I explained that my marriage had failed. How the tables had turned.

When we live our lives with a judgmental finger pointed outward, dealing out condemnation and accusations on those around us, we run a terrible risk of executing judgment on ourselves—sometimes in the very areas in which we are judging. I've seen this in myself too often. I have noticed that it happens less frequently as I draw closer to God, but I still struggle. I have felt irritated with men who gawk at women walking by like they're sexual objects, yet I have looked at pornography. I have frowned on people who cheat God by not tithing, but I have caught myself cheating the government by stretching the truth when completing my income taxes. I have dealt harshly with my children for doing certain things—the very things that I have done myself. I could go on and on about my own failures in judging others.

Praise be to God that all of us can receive mercy for our sins if we are not hypocritical and do not accuse others of similar sins. Jesus says that whatever standard of measure we use to judge others will be used against us. A standard of harshness will not work in our favor. But if we have a standard of mercy, compassion, and understanding, then we have the confidence of knowing that the same standard will be used for us by God.

We often see this balance play out naturally in our relationships. People tend to be treated like they treat others, as illustrated in one of my favorite movies, *It's a Wonderful Life*. The main character,

George Bailey, treats everyone in town with respect and compassion as he loans money at reasonable rates, forsaking opportunities of becoming wealthy. When poor George needs someone to save him from a disastrous error at his Building and Loan, the entire town comes together to show the same kindness and compassion. I am so moved by the ending of that movie that I can't stop crying. I imagine it's much like the grace that God shows someone who is humble.

SELF-JUDGMENT

Jesus's teaching on judgment was also illustrated fatally in the life of David, the king of Israel, a man after God's own heart. Many of us know of David's adulterous relationship with a woman named Bathsheba, but it was his harsh judgment toward another man that began a series of events that punished David for his sins.

When the story opens in 2 Samuel 11, we see that David has only positive narratives up to this point in Scripture, from his defeat of a giant named Goliath to his kindness toward Mephibosheth, the grandson of King Saul. He shows strength in battle, mercy toward God's anointed, wisdom as a leader, and a desire to seek God with all his heart. David's stock is soaring! He will become the standard for all kings after him, and God makes a covenant with him that someone from his lineage will always reign as king.

But when David stays back in Jerusalem while his armies are in battle, things take a turn. David observes a beautiful wife named Bathsheba bathing and decides that he wants her for himself. It doesn't seem to matter that she is the wife of Uriah, one of his particularly noble warriors. David calls for Bathsheba and sleeps with her, and she stays with him in his palace quarters for several days. Bathsheba goes back home, and I imagine that David assumes no consequences will come of the affair.

Later, however, Bathsheba sends a disturbing note to David that she is pregnant. David is shrewd and has a plan to cover up the sin:

he calls Uriah home from the battle and encourages him to enjoy a romantic night with his beautiful bride. David knows that men long to be with their wives after a stretch of time away, and his plan could save David's reputation by giving the appearance that Uriah fathered the child. But Uriah is a different sort of man. He refuses to be with his wife because his heart and mind are with the men on the battlefield. It would be disrespectful to eat, drink, and be merry at a time like this, despite David's attempts to change his mind using words and wine.

David decides to send Uriah back into battle so that he will die. He is so bent on hiding his adultery that he orders the captain to send Uriah into the fiercest fighting and then to withdraw all support for him and watch him die. It's a despicable action that I would expect only from the worst of dictators. A sin rooted in envy and pride has grown to adultery and now murder.

After Uriah dies, David seems to have solved his problem. He's free to marry Bathsheba, and by moving quickly, he is able to not only cover up the pregnancy but also appear as Bathsheba's savior. Culturally, David is taking a grieving widow into his wealthy establishment. To the casual, unsuspecting observer, he appears as a gracious and wonderful man. Though things had gotten out of hand, David must be relieved that he has saved and even enhanced his reputation, gained the affections of a beautiful woman, and received no punishment for his obvious sins against God, Uriah, and Bathsheba.

But one man, Nathan the prophet, is not fooled. David can't get away with skeletons in his closet when a prophet is in his midst! Nathan approaches David with an allegorical story about a poor man and his only prized possession, a small lamb. He tells how the poor man loved the lamb and nursed it from youth, but a rich man stole it and served it as the main course to a stranger. The rich man had many lambs of his own and chose instead to steal from the poor man. David is very disturbed by Nathan's story of injustice and becomes angry, announcing with full fervor that the rich man deserved to die, and should pay *four times* for the lamb.

Nathan stuns David by responding in 2 Samuel 12:7: "You are the man!" David didn't realize that Nathan was telling the story about Uriah and his wife. David had shown hypocrisy in his judgmental rage, failing to recognize the tragedy of the death of a noble warrior and the violation of the marriage covenant. His sin has blinded him, and he has further sinned by judging.

The progression of David's sin is worthy of a study in its own right. David first sins by failing to lead his men in battle, perhaps in selfishness, arrogance, or downright laziness. Then David lusts after a woman who is not his own. Then he commits adultery. Then David lacks humility by attempting to protect his reputation by covering up the affair. He also attempts to place the responsibility of raising his own child on someone else. David then assures the killing of a man who has shown no treachery, only loyalty to him and his troops. David shows pride again as he marries Bathsheba and improves his reputation while basking in his successful cover-up.

All these things happen with no apparent consequences, at least not immediately. David's sins—and his hypocrisy—are now fully in the open when he rages against and judges a man in a fictional story who has committed a far lesser evil. He will now face his own judgment: paying four times the price, as he deserved to die.

DAVID'S FOURFOLD PAYMENT

It's impossible to know for certain, but if David had repented of his sins against God, Uriah, and Bathsheba before Nathan confronted him, it's possible that God would have dealt with David compassionately and mercifully. We serve a merciful and loving God who is just to forgive our sins when we confess them (1 John 1:9). But David is not humbled—and even has the audacity to judge another—until Nathan speaks to him and dramatically proclaims his hypocrisy. Nathan lays out a punishment that addresses each of David's sins, an eye-for-an-eye retribution that starts with his murder and adultery.

> Why have you despised the word of the Lord by doing evil in His sight? You have struck down Uriah the Hittite with the sword, have taken his wife to be your wife, and have killed him with the sword of the sons of Ammon. Now therefore, the sword shall never depart from your house, because you have despised Me and have taken the wife of Uriah the Hittite to be your wife. Thus says the Lord, "Behold, I will raise up evil against you from your own household; I will even take your wives before your eyes and give them to your companion, and he will lie with your wives in broad daylight. Indeed you did it secretly, but I will do this thing before all Israel, and under the sun." (2 Samuel 12:9–12)

God brings violence to David through his own household because he brought violence on his faithful fighting man. Similarly, David will see adultery against his own wives as punishment for committing adultery himself. And as unmerciful as these punishments are, the worst is what follows: the death of four of his sons, the "four times" punishment for his judgment of the fictional man in Nathan's story.

INFANT SON OF BATHSHEBA

The immediate consequence of David's sin is an unplanned pregnancy. After Nathan confronts David with his sin, David acknowledges his error.

> Then David said to Nathan, "I have sinned against the Lord." And Nathan said to David, "The Lord also has taken away your sin; you shall not die. However, because by this deed you have given occasion to the enemies of the Lord to blaspheme, the child also that is born to you shall surely die." (2 Samuel 12:13–14)

Though David fasts and pleads for his son, the baby dies. It's terrible that an innocent baby's life is taken as part of the consequence of David's sin. This sounds like a great injustice, and it happens every day in our world. An innocent baby often takes the punishment for the sins of the father or mother. It's hard to fathom but is often the way of things: innocent blood is shed for the guilt of the sinner. It is God's way. In fact, it is the way that He creates salvation: God's innocent, perfect Son also died because of sinners. Jesus didn't deserve the punishment, just like David's son didn't deserve to die. Yet you and I somehow are cleared of our guilt. The next time we see injustice and innocent blood shed in our world, consider how God makes it all right in the raising of the dead. He did it with Christ. He'll do it again.

Innocent blood is shed for the guilt of the sinner. It is God's way.

AMNON

The death of David's first son with Bathsheba is unmistakably tied to his sin with Bathsheba. But the violence doesn't stop there. One by one, the Bible begins to describe stories involving the rest of David's sons and the fulfillment of Nathan's prophecy. It's not a coincidence that David condemned a fictitious man in Nathan's story to a fourfold repayment and then there are four stories of the death of four sons.

The second story tells about Amnon, the son of David with his second wife. Amnon had a crush on his half sister, Tamar, and tricked her into being alone with him. He raped her, and he then compounded his wickedness by treating her with shame and disgust afterward. Amnon is killed in vengeance two years later by Tamar's full brother, Absalom (2 Samuel 13).

ABSALOM

Absalom, the son of David and another wife, Maacah, rebelled against David and stole the kingdom. One of his first acts of treachery to establish himself as king was to sleep with all of David's concubines who were left behind when David fled. In fulfillment of Nathan's prophecy, the acts were performed in a tent on the roof of David's house, and all of the city knew that Absalom showed contempt for his father. Absalom is killed in a later battle when David's commander finds him tangled in tree branches due to his excessively long hair (2 Samuel 18).

ADONIJAH

Adonijah, the son of David and another wife, also rebelled against David in his old age. Before David's death, Adonijah sought to steal the kingdom from David's other son Solomon. When his attempt backfired, Adonijah tried to gain control of David's beautiful nurse, who would ultimately become the wife of Solomon and likely the object of his affection in the book Song of Solomon. This pushes Solomon to execute Adonijah (1 Kings 2).

DAVID'S REPENTANCE

David's sin is very great, but God's mercy is even greater. David repents of his sin, and even though he still bears the consequences, Nathan says he is forgiven. David's plea of repentance is recorded in Psalm 51.

> Be gracious to me, O God, according to Your lovingkindness;
> According to the greatness of Your compassion blot out
>   my transgressions.
> Wash me thoroughly from my iniquity
> And cleanse me from my sin.
> For I know my transgressions,
> And my sin is ever before me.
> Against You, You only, I have sinned
> And done what is evil in Your sight,
> So that You are justified when You speak
> And blameless when You judge.

Behold, I was brought forth in iniquity,
And in sin my mother conceived me.
Behold, You desire truth in the innermost being,
And in the hidden part You will make me know wisdom.
Purify me with hyssop, and I shall be clean;
Wash me, and I shall be whiter than snow.
Make me to hear joy and gladness,
Let the bones which You have broken rejoice.
Hide Your face from my sins
And blot out all my iniquities.

Create in me a clean heart, O God,
And renew a steadfast spirit within me.
Do not cast me away from Your presence
And do not take Your Holy Spirit from me.
Restore to me the joy of Your salvation
And sustain me with a willing spirit.
Then I will teach transgressors Your ways,
And sinners will be converted to You.

Deliver me from bloodguiltiness, O God, the God of
  my salvation;
Then my tongue will joyfully sing of Your righteousness.
O Lord, open my lips,
That my mouth may declare Your praise.
For You do not delight in sacrifice, otherwise I would give it;
You are not pleased with burnt offering.
The sacrifices of God are a broken spirit;
A broken and a contrite heart, O God,
You will not despise.

By Your favor do good to Zion;
Build the walls of Jerusalem.
Then You will delight in righteous sacrifices,

In burnt offering and whole burnt offering;
Then young bulls will be offered on Your altar.
(Psalm 51:1–19)

What a poetic expression of the waves of David's emotions. David uses four different words to describe his fault: transgression, sin, iniquity, and bloodguiltiness. He appears to understand the gravity of his wrongdoing, and he confesses his need for God's grace, cleansing, and renewal. In his extreme emotion, David exaggerates about sinning only against God and grieves all his sins, even from conception and in childbirth. His illogical statements are akin to saying all-or-nothing phrases like "no one has ever loved me" or "I wish I'd never been born."

Despite his over-the-top perspective, I hope you and I can grasp the gravity of our sins like David did, grieving our sin of judging others when we are just as guilty ourselves. May we repent and change our countenance from that of outward judgment to inward repentance. If you struggle with what words to say to God as you repent, read Psalm 51 to guide your heart.

CHURCH DISCIPLINE

David's story is a tragic illustration of Jesus's warning not to judge. But how do we balance this with the call to judge believers who commit sin and correct them with the word of God? In 2 Timothy 3:16-17, we learn that all Scripture is inspired by God and is useful to teach us what is true and to make us realize what is wrong in our lives. It corrects us when we are wrong and teaches us to do what is right. Indeed, all Scripture is inspired by God and profitable for teaching, reproof, correction, and training in righteousness, but Jesus teaches us that in the way we judge, we will be judged. We should be merciful, compassionate, and understanding in our judgment if we wish to be treated in the same way.

Therefore, our instruction is not to suddenly refuse to ever call out sin or acknowledge a person's immorality. Jesus is clear that there is a process in handling wrongdoing in the body of Christ.

> If your brother sins, go and show him his fault in private; if he listens to you, you have won your brother. But if he does not listen to you, take one or two more with you, so that by the mouth of two or three witnesses every fact may be confirmed. If he refuses to listen to them, tell it to the church; and if he refuses to listen even to the church, let him be to you as a Gentile and a tax collector. (Matthew 18:15-17)

The process has built-in patience and understanding. The first step is to privately approach a fellow brother and attempt to get him to listen. This respects the brother so as not to publicly shame him, and it falls short of condemnation. The context of this passage is in regard to forgiveness, so the purpose of church discipline is for the brother to see his fault, be won over, and be forgiven. The first step is followed by more opportunities to convince the brother of repentance, a very deliberate effort to win back the brother in Christ. Condemnation is completely undesirable.

This process applies only to our fellow brothers and sisters in Christ. What about those of the world? Is it appropriate to judge the sins of the nonbelievers in our society? Paul addresses this question in his letter to the Corinthians.

> I wrote you in my letter not to associate with immoral people; I did not at all mean with the immoral people of this world, or with the covetous and swindlers, or with idolaters, for then you would have to go out of the world. But actually, I wrote to you not to associate with any so-called brother if he is an immoral person, or covetous, or an idolater, or a reviler, or a drunkard, or a swindler—not even to eat with such a one. For what have I to do with judging outsiders? Do you not judge those who are

within the church? But those who are outside, God judges. (1 Corinthians 5:9–13)

We are not to judge those outside the body of Christ. They are not under the yoke of Jesus and therefore cannot be expected to live by the same faith and follow the same teachings as Christians. Condemnation is not part of the process for approaching fellow believers—and it has no place in our relationship with the rest of the world.

For judgment will be merciless to one who has shown no mercy; mercy triumphs over judgment. (James 2:13)

Do not be mistaken: this is not abdicating God's moral authority over society. It is correct to stand firm on biblical principles and seek to influence society to align with God's standards. But you and I have no authority to define right and wrong and certainly no standing to condemn. Our hope is to have all people acknowledge their sins, be received by the Lord in repentance, and come to the knowledge of the truth that Jesus's death and resurrection cleanses them of sin.

ADULTEROUS WOMAN

Ultimately, mercy triumphs over judgment. James 2:13 says, "For judgment will be merciless to one who has shown no mercy; mercy triumphs over judgment." In talking with an adulterous woman, Jesus illustrates how to show mercy without compromising the truth of God's standard for righteousness.

John 8 tells us that Jesus is teaching in the temple when the scribes and the Pharisees set an adulterous woman in the courtyard. They challenge Jesus: "Now in the Law Moses commanded us to stone such women; what then do You say?" (John 8:5). The woman was caught in the very act, and the Pharisees are seeking to trap Jesus, too. If Jesus shows mercy, He may appear to be rejecting the Law and will be judged as a heretic. If he shows judgment, He will appear double-minded in His teaching and lose followers.

But Jesus does not fall into the trap. Instead, he pauses and writes in the sand. We don't know what is written, but it seems to make a difference. The Pharisees become persistent, expecting a response. Jesus stands and says, "He who is without sin among you, let him be the first to throw a stone at her" (John 8:7). Jesus goes back to writing in the sand, and one by one, the men who were ready to condemn the woman begin to walk away, the older men followed by the younger men. They are all convicted that they are not without sin.

> Straightening up, Jesus said to her, "Woman, where are they? Did no one condemn you?" She said, "No one, Lord." And Jesus said, "I do not condemn you, either. Go. From now on sin no more." (John 8:10–11)

Jesus is merciful to the woman. He does not make excuses for her actions, and He doesn't avoid calling sin for what it is. But he doesn't condemn her; He protects her from condemnation. He gives her an opportunity to sin no more.

This is how I want Jesus to treat me. And this is how He would have me treat others. I pray we follow Him. May we no longer judge with condemnation and hate but strive to show God's mercy and compassion.

---

*May we no longer judge with condemnation
and hate but strive to show God's mercy and compassion.*

REFLECTION ON
JUDGING OTHERS

Judge Not
Jesus says that whatever standard of measure we use to judge others will be used against us. When dealing with others, do you tend to use a standard of criticism and harshness or a standard of mercy and compassion?

Self-Judgment
We see in 2 Samuel the progression of David's sins of lust, adultery, and murder. However, it's David's hypocritical judgment that serves as the most damning evidence, prompting Nathan to call out his sinful nature. Have you ever judged others in the same ways that you have sinned? How?

David's Fourfold Payment
Nathan lays out the eye-for-an-eye consequences that David will receive for his sins: the deaths of his four sons. Do you believe God's wrath is always fair? Do you believe His mercy is always fair?

David's Repentance
David records an emotional plea of repentance in Psalm 51. Has God brought to your attention any hypocrisy in your life?

Church Discipline
The Bible provides a clear process for addressing wrongdoing by other believers. What have been your experiences in approaching other believers about their sins? If you've been approached by another believer about your own sin, were you receptive to the discipline?

Adulterous Woman
Jesus reveals God's character when He shows mercy rather than judgment to an adulterous woman. He does not excuse her actions, but He also does not condemn her. Instead, He gives her an opportunity to sin no more. How has God shown you mercy rather than judgment? How have you used the opportunity to sin no more?

OH GOD, WHY CAN'T I STOP
Holding On to Bitterness

WHEN I FIRST MET my wife, she shared her story of divorce. She had been faithfully married to her high school sweetheart, with whom she had two little boys and a comfortable home. Though she had no relationship with God and dismissed His existence, she thought she had it all. She felt safe and happy—until the day her husband asked for a divorce.

Suddenly, life as she knew it was gone. When her husband left, so did her sense of security and worth. She looked around in shock at her baby and her preschooler, and she felt utterly lost. At first, she found relief in well-meaning family and friends who expressed the bewilderment and anger that she could not articulate. But she found no solid place to stand and began to sink into bitterness.

One day, she hit bottom. She was sitting alone on an outdoor bench, reflecting on her circumstances, when she was overcome by despair. Despite the sunny sky, she dropped to her knees in darkness and hopelessness. She did not know God at the time, but she had nowhere else to turn. She cried out in fear.

When things go tremendously wrong, how can we avoid becoming bitter with disappointment and anger?

THE BOOK OF RUTH

There is a gem of a story in the Bible about a woman named Ruth that holds some answers for us. It is historically set in what I consider the dark ages of Israeli history, the period of the Judges. It's a story of redemption and healing of bitterness for Ruth's mother-in-law, Naomi, in the disguise of a romantic drama.

Ruth is introduced to us as a Moabite, which means that she was born of a people who originated from an incestuous relationship. The disturbing beginning of the Moabite people is documented in Genesis 19, after God destroyed the immoral cities of Sodom and Gomorrah and allowed a man named Lot to escape with his two daughters. Isolated in the mountains and fearing they'd never have families of their own, Lot's daughters devised a plan to have children with their father.

> Then the firstborn said to the younger, "Our father is old, and there is not a man on earth to come in to us after the manner of the earth. Come, let us make our father drink wine, and let us lie with him that we may preserve our family through our father." So they made their father drink wine that night, and the firstborn went in and lay with her father; and he did not know when she lay down or when she arose. On the following day, the firstborn said to the younger, "Behold, I lay last night with my father; let us make him drink wine tonight also; then you go in and lie with him, that we may preserve our family through our father." So they made their father drink wine that night also, and the younger arose and lay with him; and he did not know when she lay down or when she arose. Thus both the daughters of Lot were with child by their father. The firstborn bore a son, and called his name Moab; he is the father of the Moabites to this day. As for the younger, she also bore a son, and called his name Ben-ammi; he is the father of the sons of Ammon to this day. (Genesis 19:31–38)

The Bible repeats six times that Ruth is a Moabitess. She is not of God's chosen people, the Israelites, but from heathens with a shameful origin. However, we will see that Ruth is the best illustration of loyalty in all the Bible. Her story reveals how she gives herself, her life, and her allegiance to a bitter, hopeless, and poor woman, Naomi. And through this loyalty, Naomi's life will be changed, displaying the redemptive power of God to conquer bitterness.

The redemptive power of God conquers bitterness.

ABANDONING GOD

The story of Ruth begins with the story of her mother-in-law, Naomi. Naomi—a name that means "pleasant or delight"—and her husband, Elimelech, decide to leave the land of Canaan. Canaan is the land that God promised to His people, the land for which God fought through his servant Joshua. But due to a famine in the land, Naomi and her husband quit and leave for Moab. God's people had stopped believing in their God, Jehovah, and were looking for better opportunities elsewhere.

But tragedy strikes in Moab. Elimelech dies, and ten years later, so do Naomi's two sons. Her sons had married Moabite women, Orpah and Ruth, but they have not yet had children. Naomi has lost her most precious assets. She is in a foreign land with no family except her two Moabite daughters-in-law, and they are faring no better without a husband or sons.

In those days, a woman needed a man—a father, husband, or son—to provide for her. Women had few opportunities to provide for themselves, resulting in many becoming servants or prostitutes. Naomi's situation illustrates one of the reasons that God repeatedly emphasizes that we are to care for widows.

Naomi is old and has little hope that she can provide another son to her daughters-in-law to keep the family line going. In despair, she instructs her daughters-in-law to go back to their families, reasoning that they are still young and can find other husbands.

> Return, my daughters! Go, for I am too old to have a husband. If I said I have hope, if I should even have a husband tonight and also bear sons, would you therefore wait until they were grown? Would you therefore refrain from marrying? No, my daughters; for it is harder for me than for you, for the hand of the Lord has gone forth against me. (Ruth 1:12–13)

Orpah agrees sadly and leaves. However, Ruth responds differently. Even though Naomi has nothing to offer Ruth, she refuses to leave her and to leave God. Ruth may merely be a Moabite, a widow, sonless, and penniless, but she is fiercely loyal to Naomi—a level of loyalty that is not often seen even in God's people.

> Ruth said, "Do not urge me to leave you or turn back from following you; for where you go, I will go, and where you lodge, I will lodge. Your people shall be my people, and your God, my God. Where you die, I will die, and there I will be buried. Thus may the Lord do to me, and worse, if anything but death parts you and me." (Ruth 1:16–17)

How often do we see fierce loyalty? Employees can no longer depend on employers for lifelong careers; spouses struggle to remain committed to their vows. One relationship in which I see this kind of loyalty is with our sports teams. Green Bay Packers fans sell out games and endure subfreezing temperatures in hopes of winning a championship. Even after years of falling short of expectations and missing out on Super Bowl victories, Green Bay Packers fans never give up on their team. But their loyalty isn't too difficult: Green Bay is still one of the best teams in football.

With some of the greatest quarterbacks of all time, they routinely make the playoffs and have several Super Bowl victories under their belt.

Ruth is different. She shows loyalty despite Naomi having nothing to offer her. This kind of loyalty is priceless. Samuel Goldwyn, the famed early 1900s filmmaker, once said, "I'll take fifty percent efficiency to get one hundred percent loyalty."[5] As a manager and leader in my industry, I couldn't agree more. One of my employees isn't the most skilled of my team or the smartest or the most experienced, but he is the most loyal. I can replace skill, intelligence, and experience, but it's almost impossible to find his kind of loyalty.

It matters perhaps nowhere greater than in marriage. When my wife and I were dating, she let me know that loyalty topped the list of qualities she sought in a mate. So when I became involved in an intense work project after we were married that involved several weeks of travel, I knew I needed to be very intentional with my actions regarding female coworkers. It didn't matter that my wife and I had been humming along with much joy: we both recognized from experience the ingredients for a potential threat. Before the project, I spoke plainly to my wife about the situation, and she admitted to feeling uneasy. I explained that I wanted nothing and no one to come between us, and we talked about the steps that I would take to remain loyal to her. She was grateful that I was fighting for our marriage. Fierce loyalty is all she wanted.

But Naomi doesn't notice the value of Ruth's loyalty. Her life has certainly turned for the worse as she grieves the tragic loss of her husband and sons. However, Naomi's grief has hardened into bitterness. She believes that God is against her. When Naomi and Ruth travel together back to Israel and some of the people call out her name in recognition, Naomi is quick to share her bitterness.

---

5. Samuel Goldwyn, *Forbes Quotes*, https://www.forbes.com/quotes/10732, accessed December 1, 2020.

> She said to them, "Do not call me Naomi; call me Mara, for the Almighty has dealt very bitterly with me. I went out full, but the Lord has brought me back empty. Why do you call me Naomi, since the Lord has witnessed against me and the Almighty has afflicted me?" (Ruth 1:20–21)

It was Naomi and her husband who had decided to leave the Promised Land and walk away from God. However, she is now blaming God for her misery. She wants to exchange her name, which means "pleasant," to be called Mara, which means "bitter." Naomi is bitter that her life lacks the blessings she enjoyed and expected.

FINDING HOPE

Despite Naomi's hardened heart, Ruth remains loyal and begins to look for a means to sustain herself and her mother-in-law. She asks Naomi's permission to collect leftover grain by gleaning in the fields, one of God's many mechanisms for providing for the poor. Landowners were commanded by law to share their resources by allowing poor people to walk behind the harvesters and pick the leftovers from the ground.

> Now when you reap the harvest of your land, you shall not reap to the very corners of your field, nor shall you gather the gleanings of your harvest. Nor shall you glean your vineyard, nor shall you gather the fallen fruit of your vineyard; you shall leave them for the needy and for the stranger. I am the Lord your God. (Leviticus 19:9–10)

God's welfare system requires the poor to work, and Ruth is a hard worker. She walks behind the harvesters, collecting and processing the raw materials. But work ethic isn't enough to protect a single woman during this dark period. The overseer calls Ruth a young "Moabite," which is likely a racist comment in these dangerous times. Judges 19 recounts a vile story from this period about mob violence toward a foreigner, gang rape of a woman, and gruesome dismemberment by a man. Ruth is a target.

It is God's providence that Ruth ends up gleaning in the fields of a landowner named Boaz. He is in the family of Naomi's deceased husband, and he is a man of wealth and respect. Boaz is obeying God's commands of allowing the poor to glean in his fields when he takes note of Ruth. He not only allows her to stay; he invites her to stay in his field, work alongside his female servants, and drink from the water jars whenever she is thirsty. He commands the men not to harm her.

Boaz treats this foreign woman with dignity and equity, a favor so unexpected that Ruth bows with her face to the ground and inquires why he gives such deference to her. Ruth recognizes that she is less than a servant but is being treated as equal to a servant. Boaz remarks at her loyalty to Naomi, that she has left her family and homeland to stay with her mother-in-law and seek refuge with the Lord. Boaz rewards Ruth's loyalty. With his blessing, Ruth works until evening before carrying home to her mother-in-law all that she has gleaned.

Throughout the book of Ruth, the contrast between the responses of Ruth and Naomi is noticeable. When Naomi's life takes a turn for the worse, she fails to see her lack of obedience to God. Though she's justified to grieve her losses, she seems to feel entitled and blames God for her circumstances. She seems resigned to a hopeless situation. In contrast, Ruth takes action, controlling what she can control. Despite her loss, she chooses to stick with God and with Naomi. She chooses to work hard. She remains humble and speaks to Boaz with no sense of entitlement. Ruth embodies the characteristics necessary to avoid bitterness: loyalty, proactive effort, and humility.

Ruth's humbleness before Boaz illustrates the humility with which we are to approach our relationship with God. Like Ruth, we are less than servants in His presence, foreigners in a way. The Scriptures say that we were objects of wrath but became adopted into His family through Christ. And because of Christ, we become not just servants of God but sons and daughters of God, coheirs with Jesus Christ. It is a grace that is truly amazing. To be coheirs with God's only begotten Son is an unfathomable blessing.

Ruth's humbleness before Boaz illustrates the humility with which we are to approach our relationship with God.

REQUESTING REDEMPTION

The bitterness and abandonment that Naomi feels begin to soften by Ruth's loyalty and Boaz's kindness. She tells Ruth to stay close to the safe protection of Boaz and his fields. Later, seeing an opportunity, Naomi becomes a bit of a matchmaker. She advises Ruth to anoint herself with perfume, put on her best clothes, and approach Boaz at the right time. I imagine this is a little like *Pride and Prejudice*, my wife's favorite love story, in which poor sisters are nudged by their scheming mother to marry wealthy men. But Ruth is as much a prize as Boaz.

That night, Ruth follows Naomi's instructions. She finds Boaz sleeping next to the harvested grain, likely to protect it from thieves, and lies quietly at his feet for some time. When he is startled awake, Ruth replies with a request.

> He said, "Who are you?" And she answered, "I am Ruth your maid. So spread your covering over your maid, for you are a close relative." (Ruth 3:9)

In so many words, Ruth is asking Boaz to marry her and redeem her for himself. She is fully submitting to him. Asking for covering in the cold of the night is not just a request to be warmed but a request to be saved. We see similar wording in a passage in Ezekiel in which God expresses His love for the city of Jerusalem and its people. It is beautiful and poetic, a picture of God's grace for his bride.

> "Then I passed by you and saw you, and behold, you were at the time for love; so I spread My skirt over you and covered your nakedness. I also swore to you and entered into a covenant with you so that you became Mine," declares the Lord GOD. (Ezekiel 16:8)

Ruth will belong to Boaz if he wants her. She has shown her loyalty to God and Naomi, and now she is offering it to Boaz. Boaz responds with one of the best compliments in all of Scripture.

> "Now, my daughter, do not fear. I will do for you whatever you ask, for all my people in the city know that you are a woman of excellence." (Ruth 3:9)

Ruth may have been just a Moabitess, but she has a new reputation. She is known to be loyal and devoted, hardworking, submissive, young, and beautiful. She is a woman of excellence. She is ready to be a bride.

RECEIVING AMAZING GRACE

Boaz wants to marry Ruth, but he has a problem. God's Word provides an opportunity for a widow to marry within the family to keep the legacy of the passing husband alive.

> When brothers live together and one of them dies and has no son, the wife of the deceased shall not be married outside the family to a strange man. Her husband's brother shall go in to her and take her to himself as wife and perform the duty of a husband's brother to her. It shall be that the firstborn whom

she bears shall assume the name of his dead brother, so that his name will not be blotted out from Israel.
(Deuteronomy 25:5–6)

It may seem strange to us that a brother or close relative would be commanded to marry a deceased man's widow. This was not a perversion or some cheap thrill for the surviving relative. In fact, it was generally viewed as an undesirable, costly obligation. Marrying the widow and providing a son required the living relative to provide for them without gaining land in the process—no "return on investment." The deceased man's land would stay in his name, with the son born from his surviving wife, even though the surviving relative conceived a son. In this time period, God's promises were rooted in the land given to all the Israelites. Thanks to this merciful provision, the dead man's name would not be blotted from history; it would live on forever.

Boaz knows that another man is a closer relative to Naomi's dead husband. According to God's Word, this man holds the responsibility of taking in Naomi and Ruth, bearing a son, and then allowing that son to take on the name and property of Naomi's late husband, Elimelech. He is obligated to be the kinsman-redeemer who ensures that the family name endures.

Boaz shows his sincere and decisive commitment to Ruth by finding the closer relative and indicating that Elimelech's property is for sale by Naomi. The man agrees to fulfill his role as the kinsman-redeemer until Boaz informs him that the responsibility includes Ruth, the Moabitess. The man refuses to jeopardize his financial security and offers the role to Boaz—exactly what Boaz wants. He is now free to take on the responsibility, care for Naomi's needs, give Elimelech an enduring name in Israel, and most importantly, win the loyal woman of excellence. Ruth the Moabitess is worthy.

The story concludes with the wedding of Boaz and Ruth, and eventually, a son. The son, Obed, is of particular significance because he is declared to be the son of Naomi, and his name means "serving, worshiping." He is the grandfather of King David and in the lineage of Jesus Christ, who is the Redeemer of all the world.

As beautiful as the ending is for Boaz and Ruth, the book of Ruth is less about their love story and more about the costly redemption of Naomi. It's so important not to miss how these events impact Naomi. She is now redeemed through the love and loyalty of her daughter-in-law, the Moabitess. The change in her circumstances is reflected in the reactions of her friends.

> Then the women said to Naomi, "Blessed is the Lord who has not left you without a redeemer today, and may his name become famous in Israel. May he also be to you a restorer of life and a sustainer of your old age; for your daughter-in-law, who loves you and is better to you than seven sons, has given birth to him." (Ruth 4:14–15)

Naomi was once so hopeless over losing her husband and two sons that she wanted to change her name to Mara. She became bitter to the point that she could not see God. Yet God loved her and gave her a loyal daughter-in-law who was better to her than seven sons, an amazing comparison in a culture and time in which sons were so necessary and coveted. But even the people could see that Ruth, with her persistent faithfulness, was the most important person in Naomi's life, better than any number of sons.

Naomi is redeemed. The bitterness is healed.

HEALING FROM BITTERNESS

In Ruth, we see a model for us of extreme and enduring loyalty, a virtue of tremendous value. May we become like Ruth, making God our Lord forever, loving our spouses and family members unconditionally, and serving our churches and employers with dedication and reliability. And when we come across someone like Ruth, may we place a premium on his or her value and do what we can to draw that person to us.

In Naomi, we see that the cure for bitterness is redemption. Some self-professed Christians, believers in the Lord who "know" that we have been redeemed, are bitter like Naomi. They have been hurt by others or by circumstances through no fault of their own, and their grief has turned to bitterness. It's understandable. Naomi felt that God was against her to allow such a tragedy, and there is no shortage of tragedies today. Some of us are dealing with betrayal, sickness, death, poverty, oppression, and injustice. There are many reasons to be bitter. It is critical to recognize that bitterness can rob us of life and ruin all joy.

But we have been redeemed. We have a Kinsman Redeemer who is even greater than Boaz: Jesus Christ. He has redeemed us with something more costly than money and land. Jesus has saved us with His precious blood that was shed on a cross. Jesus has more reason to be bitter than anyone. His blood was shed at the hands of betrayal, hatred, and injustice. But he hung on a cross, nails hammered into his hands and feet, and said, "Father, forgive them, for they do not know what they are doing" (Luke 23:34).

We have the ultimate Kinsman Redeemer in Jesus Christ.

In the same way that Boaz redeemed Naomi from her situation, Christ redeemed us. We were lost and morally bankrupt, some people hurt to the point of anger and bitterness. And through Christ, we are saved. The wrongs, hurts, and pains that we have endured—and inflicted—in this life are reconciled by Jesus's death on the cross and redeemed through His resurrection. We are saved into eternal life with our heavenly Father, with a promise that one day He will wipe away every tear. Christ's redemption into a new and everlasting life is worth seven times more than our losses.

My wife has experienced the redemption of Christ. In the devastating wake of her failed marriage, she struggled with the bitterness of betrayal until a pivotal phone call with a Christian friend. Her friend listened to her pain, then responded in a most unexpected way.

"I'll pray for your husband," she said.

This was different, opposite of all of the other reactions of friends and family. My wife thought, I'm the one who's been betrayed. I'm the one who is hurting. She asked, "Why would you pray for him?"

Her friend knew that redemption is the only way to heal. She introduced my wife to God's mercy and grace, His unconditional love for both her and her husband. What unconventional wisdom! God's wisdom often seems upside down in this world.

That phone call was a turning point for my wife. She couldn't shake the peculiar words of her friend, so she began to journey through the Bible to make sense of the perspective. For a long time, she didn't understand God's ways. She asked questions, expressed her frustrations, and doubted His sovereignty. Ultimately, my wife came to know the great Redeemer, Jesus, and yielded to His Word. What happened was amazing: she accepted the need for a Savior and placed her faith in Jesus as the risen Lord.

Today, God has restored the pieces of my wife's life. She has found love in a second marriage, fulfillment in a new career, and comfort in a different home. The pain of her failed marriage is not erased, but much of the brokenness and bitterness has healed. In fact, she appreciates her pain, because it is the means through which she has discovered the joy of salvation. As she has continued to love the Lord and receive His grace, the less she dwells on what she has lost. What she has gained in Christ is so much greater.

She is redeemed.

REFLECTION ON
HOLDING ON TO BITTERNESS

The Book of Ruth
Ruth is a foreigner who comes from a people with a shameful origin, yet she is not defined by these things. Ruth exemplifies the virtue of loyalty, and Boaz recognizes her as a "woman of excellence." Is there an aspect of your identity that you should no longer allow to define you?

Abandoning God
Naomi blames God for the tragic loss of her husband and two sons. However, she doesn't recognize her role in walking away from God and the Promised Land. Have any of your decisions played a role in your loss and bitterness?

Finding Hope
Although Ruth is less than a servant, Boaz treats her with dignity and respect. Ruth responds to his unexpected favor with humility and gratitude. Like Ruth, we have been welcomed into God's family with unmerited favor. We are more than servants; we are adopted as sons and daughters of God, coheirs with Christ. How do you perceive God and respond to your relationship with Him?

Requesting Redemption

When Naomi recognizes in Boaz an opportunity to change the circumstances, she advises Ruth to approach Boaz and request redemption. You may not have someone like Ruth helping you through bitterness, but you do have a redeemer like Boaz in Jesus. Have you approached your Kinsman-Redeemer with a bold request to be saved?

Receiving Amazing Grace

The once-bitter Naomi is redeemed into a new life. Her friends praise the loyalty of her daughter-in-law, who they say is more valuable than seven sons. If you struggle with bitterness, have you compared your losses to your gains in the promise of redemption and abundant life in Christ?

Healing from Bitterness

Ruth is the epitome of enduring loyalty. How do you actively cultivate loyalty in yourself and place value on it in others? In contrast, Naomi illustrates bitterness throughout much of the story. In what areas of your life do you need healing from bitterness?

OH GOD, WHY CAN'T I STOP
Lusting

YOUR TYPICAL DAY MAY include many sexual temptations. A billboard on the drive to work might advertise adult entertainment. Your news feed invites you to check out attractive singles nearby. A flirty coworker asks to meet for lunch. A magazine at the dentist's office boasts first-date sex tips. An evening TV show glorifies a forbidden relationship. And late-night browsing on the internet opens the door to a porn site. Day after day, we're bombarded by an oversexualized culture.

Sexual desire should not be hidden, ignored, or condemned. It is normal and natural, created by God, the mechanism for men and women to be joined in intimacy, to become one flesh. But its power is evident in the world around us. Our culture and media glorify it graphically, intentionally, and casually, all of which make it difficult to navigate sexual temptation—including for God's people.

When I came to the Lord as a young man, I was a new creation. I no longer felt powerless against the continual lusting of women. Although I hadn't had one-night stands and casual sexual relationships, I hadn't controlled urges that I knew were wrong, and I had harmed some friendships. I had been hurt by women who only wanted casual sex and not a more intimate relationship. But the cloud of guilt and shame hovering over me—and my sense of weakness and powerlessness—was lifted when I was born again in Christ.

I put on His clothes of righteousness, and I was made new. As Romans 8:37 says, I was an overwhelming conqueror. My fresh start with the power of God gave me a new opportunity to defend against lustful desires. And I was successful . . . at first. In the first several years of my walk with the Lord, I felt rid of sexual sins and temptations. I stopped submitting to my lusts and had purity in Christ.

But there was a problem: I still lusted in my heart and with my eyes. I was easily distracted by women in the workplace, on TV, through the internet, and even at church. I asked, "God, why can't I stop lusting?"

Though you and I believe in Jesus as the sacrifice for our sins and are filled with the Holy Spirit, we are not yet in our heavenly, eternal bodies. One day we won't have the temptations of the flesh, but today we still have our bodies and the sinful desires that wage war against our souls (1 Peter 2:11). And it is a war. A study by the Institute of Family Studies found that 20 percent of men and 13 percent of women admit to cheating on their spouses in America.[6] For people under forty years old, the gap is closing as more women admit to affairs. Lust and adultery are realities for both men and women.

In this chapter, we'll focus on how preventive maintenance protects us from sin. Depending on the type of work you do, you may be familiar with problem reporting and root cause analysis. When a problem arises, you determine the root cause, then you take corrective action: immediate, interim, and permanent. Unfortunately, what often gets missed is preventive maintenance. But prevention is necessary if we want to avoid future problems. Let's look at the Old Testament stories of two brothers, Judah and Joseph, each of whom handled sexual temptation differently. One took a path toward sexual sin, the other

---

6. Wendy Wang, "Who Cheats More? The Demographics of Infidelity in America," *Institute for Family Studies*, January 10, 2018, https://ifstudies.org/blog/who-cheats-more-the-demographics-of-cheating-in-america.

toward sexual purity. From this study in contrasts, we can observe important factors and learn helpful strategies in dealing with lust.

Though our study could be taken as one of corrective action, it's not meant to be that way. The only true corrective action is forgiveness and cleansing by Jesus. Thereafter, repentance is the interim action, and our change of heart is the permanent action.

PREVENTION FOR SPECTATORS

Jesus was betrayed by one of his closest followers; He was deserted by most of his closest friends; He was falsely accused; He was found guilty in an illegal trial; He was mocked and ridiculed; He was struck; He was severely flogged; and He was nailed to a torturous cross. Yet before He died, He said, "Father, forgive them; for they do not know what they are doing" (Luke 23:34). I am still amazed, and hope to always be amazed, at the incredible forgiveness that Jesus offered during such trauma. He is truly God, for no man could be so gracious.

Indeed, the Bible is full of stories of God, both Old Testament Jehovah and New Testament Jesus, and His forgiveness. But surprisingly, there are very few stories of men forgiving other men. There is only one story that separates itself as such, and that is Joseph forgiving his ten brothers for the evil done to him.

Joseph was the respectable son of Jacob but was also favored by him. This put him above his older brothers, who came to despise him. They were going to kill him and cover up their sin, but instead threw him in an empty well and later sold him into slavery and reported to a grieving father that he had been killed by a wild animal.

Joseph had a strange turn of events in Egypt where he became head slave of a powerful man but then was falsely accused by that man's wife and was thrown into prison. He stayed there two years before God set the stage to deliver Joseph. The Pharaoh had a disturbing dream, and he sought Joseph for an interpretation. God revealed to Joseph that Egypt would have plenty for seven years but then extreme famine for seven more.

Pharaoh put Joseph in charge of food for the fourteen years. He managed the excess such that there was plenty of food for the famine and for selling to other nations (can you say global economic dominance?). This made Joseph very successful and powerful. But Joseph's true character was yet to be revealed.

His family suffered in the famine, and they heard that Egypt had food. The brothers traveled to Egypt to buy food and encountered their powerful but unrecognized younger brother. Joseph played a game with them to ensure that he would have an opportunity to see his younger brother, Benjamin, who was not involved in the earlier treachery, and his father, Jacob. Joseph revealed himself to his brothers, but instead of using his power to exact revenge, he forgave them and said that what they had meant for evil, God used for good.

Joseph is in many ways one of the types of Christ in the Bible. I have read twenty-one unique similarities between him and Jesus. From such a man, we can learn much about forgiveness, integrity, and, in this chapter, sexual purity. Genesis 37–50 are focused on Joseph (thirteen solid chapters on this man—few in the Bible have more written of them), but in the midst of these chapters is one dedicated to Judah, one of Joseph's older brothers. Genesis 38 and 39 are a study in contrasts as Judah takes a path to sexual sin while Joseph takes a path to sexual purity. We get to be spectators of these two men and how they handled sexual temptation.

JUDAH'S FAILURE

Judah is the fourth of twelve sons of the Old Testament patriarch Jacob. In Genesis 38, we see Judah venture out on his own toward a path of sexual sin. Throughout his story, we can observe five factors that drive him and his family to sin, some of which feed his lust.

INCOMPATIBLE FAITH

From the start, Judah's lusts carry him immediately to a place where he doesn't belong: falling in love with someone who doesn't share his own faith. He marries a Canaanite woman with whom he has three sons, Er, Onan, and Shelah. His marriage would have been frowned upon because the Canaanites were enemies of God who worshiped false gods.

It's important that we limit our pursuits for a mate to people of common beliefs in God. Paul writes to the Corinthians, "Do not be bound together with unbelievers; for what partnership have righteousness and lawlessness, or what fellowship has light with darkness?" (2 Corinthians 6:14). This is more than checking the box that someone believes in God. It is not just about going to church. A potential partner who genuinely believes in Christ for salvation will submit to Jesus as the authority in every part of life. Jesus will determine how he or she works, serves, manages money, manages time, makes friends, and consumes entertainment. We must guard against falling in love with someone without first determining compatibility in faith. This means not going on dates with unbelievers so that we can protect our hearts from romantic emotions for those outside the body of Christ.

GREED

The next sin we observe is the way Judah's middle son, Onan, treats Tamar, the wife of his oldest son, Er. In keeping with tradition, Tamar had been given to Onan after Er died due to his own wickedness. In ancient times, a man's name, property, and inheritance would pass down to his sons, but if a man died without sons, the closest surviving male in the family was obligated to take in the widow of his brother and raise a son to maintain that bloodline.

Despite his obligation, Onan had sex with Tamar but did not want to get her pregnant. He knew how Judah's inheritance would one day be split among the brothers: Er would have received a double portion if he had been alive, and Onan and Shelah would have each received one portion. Now that Er has died, the entire inheritance would be split between the two surviving brothers. But if Er's wife conceived a son through Onan, then that son would eventually break off and take Er's double portion with him. Onan would raise a son on Er's behalf but still be left with only one portion of the inheritance.

Therefore, when Onan has sex with Tamar, he spills his seed on the ground instead of in Tamar's womb. He wants more of the inheritance without the burdens of a wife or a son, which would have been a blessing for Tamar. Onan's selfish actions were wickedness in God's eyes, so Onan died for his greed.

LACK OF SENSITIVITY AND DISCERNMENT

By this point, Judah has endured grievous losses. He has lost his two oldest sons, Er and Onan, and still has no grandchildren. But his next move is inexcusable: Judah concludes that Tamar is somehow the cause of the deaths of his sons and sends her back home to her family. Tamar has just lost her husband, had sex with a brother-in-law who had no intention to care for her before also dying, and now her father-in-law shows no compassion. I imagine she feels used, alone, and unwanted.

Not only is Judah insensitive to Tamar, but he lacks discernment regarding his own sons. Neither Er nor Onan died because Tamar was some sort of bad luck. They died due to their own sins, which were judged by God. As a parent, the lesson from Judah's failure is to never assume that our own kids aren't capable of sin. Our children are precious to us, but they are still sinners.

Not only is Tamar innocent of the deaths of Er and Onan, but she is also patient and shows restraint. In that culture, women without husbands had few options and would likely take any man who would show interest. But Tamar does not make herself available to others. She waits a considerable amount of time for her deceased husband's youngest brother, Shelah, her rightful husband and the man who could one day provide her with children.

VICTIM MENTALITY

The story continues when Tamar hears that Judah and Shelah are taking sheep into town to be sheared. Tamar knows that Shelah is of age, and she veils herself and goes to the city gates. It's not clear why she veils herself, but Judah fails to recognize her and has no intent to give Shelah to her in marriage. Instead, he mistakes her for a prostitute and wants to sleep with her.

Judah is likely tempted to sin because he is acting out as a victim. At this point in the story, his wife has passed away. While we can sympathize with him for no longer having his wife nor the intimacy of sex in marriage, his situation does not justify his actions. Tamar is "wrapped" (Genesis 38:14), which means she is unlikely showing skin to seduce a man, so Judah is not being pursued but is being tempted from within. I imagine he is thinking: "I'm lonely. I've lost love. I need comfort. I'm away from home, and I simply want it." When we are tempted to sin, let us recognize the conversations that we have with ourselves and root out a victim mentality that tries to justify sin.

FOOLISHNESS

Judah requests sex without knowing he is approaching his daughter-in-law. He offers a goat as payment, which he must fetch from the herd. As a pledge, Tamar asks for his seal, staff, and cord, valuables that also could be used to confirm his identity. He foolishly gives them to her, has intercourse with her, and unknowingly gets her pregnant. Afterward, Judah sends the goat as payment and expects to receive his items back, but Tamar disappears.

Months later, Tamar is discovered to be pregnant and receives condemnation from many. Among the condemners is Judah, who demands to be brought to her so that she can be burned to death for fooling around and getting pregnant. What a hypocrite! He judges her for a sexual sin that he also has committed.

However, Tamar holds the cards. She sends the seal, staff, and cord to Judah for inspection, explaining that the owner of these valuables is the father. Judah immediately recognizes his belongings, admits his sin, and finally works to make things right for Tamar.

Sometimes, unfortunately, a person needs to experience the consequences of lusting to address the issue. Judah had attached himself to a woman who was not in faith. He had selfish sons and didn't recognize their faults. He was insensitive to a woman dealing with a difficult situation and emotions. He played the victim card. All of these decisions factor into his giving into lust, resulting in life-changing consequences.

In contrast to Judah, his brother resists the temptation of lust.

JOSEPH'S SUCCESS

Right after Judah's failure, which is a story of what *not* to do, is a tale about his brother, Joseph, who successfully managed temptation. The writer of Genesis seems to have been intentional about the placement of these two contrasting stories for us. God's Word has so much intelligence and structure that it's very unlikely to be coincidence. As we follow the story of Joseph, we'll learn how Joseph prevents sexual immorality.

GOD'S GRACE

In Genesis 39, we find Joseph in the home of Potiphar, a high-ranking official to Pharaoh, the king of Egypt. He has suffered betrayal and exile at the hands of his brothers and has been sold into slavery. However, even in slavery, the Bible tells us that the Lord is with Joseph. It's comforting to know that God is still there providing hope in the worst of situations. He doesn't always and immediately save us from peril, but God works out all things for good for those who love the Lord (Romans 8:28).

With God's grace, Joseph becomes a diligent worker in serving Potiphar and his home. He is eventually entrusted as Potiphar's personal servant and overseer of the entire household. The increasing success is all due to God's blessings on Joseph, and Potiphar enjoys much of this blessing. It's to our benefit to find people who love the Lord and are blessed because often the blessings overflow to everyone in their path.

DILIGENT LABOR

We can infer that Joseph is a trustworthy servant. Potiphar is a powerful Egyptian man, yet he chooses to elevate a Hebrew slave to run his entire household. When we work, we should prove ourselves as good workers, trustworthy and honorable regardless of the employer or career. Colossians 3:23-24 says this: "Whatever you do, do your work heartily, as for the Lord rather than for men, knowing that from the Lord you will receive the reward of the inheritance. It is the Lord Christ whom you serve."

Joseph exemplifies the fulfillment of this passage centuries before it was written. A person of honor and integrity receives blessings from the Lord and also eliminates many of the temptations that could otherwise materialize.

A person of honor and integrity receives blessings from the Lord and also eliminates many of the temptations that could otherwise materialize.

WILLINGNESS TO FLEE

Unfortunately, Joseph's diligence does not eliminate all temptations. Although Joseph doesn't go looking for trouble, it still comes looking for him—in the form of Potiphar's wife.

Potiphar's wife attempts to seduce the young, attractive slave and without ambiguity: she demands that he sleep with her. And not just once. She tempts him day after day after day. A man may be able to resist temptation once or twice on his own strength, but repeatedly pushing back against sexual temptation takes supernatural strength. Those who live according to God's Word must not only prevent actively seeking temptation; we must also be prepared for temptation that comes looking for us as it does for Joseph.

To address this temptation, Joseph gives three reasons to Potiphar's wife on why he cannot sleep with her. First, he cannot sin against his master. Potiphar has entrusted him with everything and only withholds his wife from him. And Joseph notes that she is withheld from him simply because she is already his wife. Second, he cannot sin against marriage. These two reasons are more than sufficient to keep him from having sex with her, but he goes on.

Third, he cannot sin against God. Even if Joseph could get away with it, he refuses to fall into this sexual relationship because it would be a great evil against God. He recognizes the ultimate authority in God.

In today's sexual revolution, God has been eliminated from the conversation. His rules, commandments, expectations, and design for sex are considered antiquated and oppressive. Joseph's refusal to comply with Potiphar's wife will have terrible consequences, but Joseph is still better off because he is right with God. We have that same choice today. If we go along with the sexual revolution, which appears to have no guidelines for propriety and purity, then we may pacify the world but do a "great evil and sin" against God, who ultimately is the only One who matters.

If we go along with the sexual revolution, then we pacify the world but sin against the only One who matters.

As the body of Christ, we must hold to a biblical view of sex and the sanctity of marriage. Many passages in the Bible reveal this view, all of which can be summed up with this: the only sex that God blesses is between a male husband and a female wife. Everything else—regardless of gender, orientation, and persuasion—is sin against God. We are all sinners who fall short of the glory of God, and we have compassion on sinners, but we must recognize the authority of God in decisions concerning sex.

In response to Joseph's repeated rejections, Potiphar's wife eventually attempts to sexually assault him. Joseph reacts with the best defense against lust. He flees! Potiphar's wife grabs his cloak, but he leaves it behind and runs naked out of the house to escape the temptation. He runs for his very life, not worrying about appearances, his reputation, or the consequences.

Grasping at an explanation for the bizarre situation, Potiphar's wife lies and claims that Joseph tried to rape her, and when she screamed, he ran out without his clothes. The lie saves her but condemns Joseph, who is thrown in jail. Although he resists sexual temptation, Joseph reaps negative consequences. He is a legitimate victim, though we know that God later works things out for the good of Joseph.

When temptation becomes more and more pervasive, the best defense is to flee. Jesus says that if your eye causes you to sin, it is better for you to gouge it out and go to heaven with one eye than to go to hell with two eyes (Matthew 5:29). It's an extreme statement to illustrate the severity of extreme temptation. When presented with recurring temptation, do something that the world would consider extreme. If you struggle with internet pornography, cancel the internet. If you're tempted to fool around when drinking, abstain from alcohol. If you're losing your ability to resist someone who is flirting with you at work, quit the job. It will be better for you and will avoid catastrophe.

WISDOM

Joseph's actions reveal a wisdom that wouldn't be written in the Bible for nearly another thousand years by the wisest man in the world, Solomon. Solomon would write warnings to his son regarding adultery and falling into sexual temptation. He gave the following instruction:

> To keep you from the evil woman,
> From the smooth tongue of the adulteress.
> Do not desire her beauty in your heart,
> Nor let her capture you with her eyelids.
> For on account of a harlot one is reduced to a loaf of bread,
> And an adulteress hunts for the precious life.
> Can a man take fire in his bosom
> And his clothes not be burned?
> Or can a man walk on hot coals
> And his feet not be scorched? (Proverbs 6:24–28)

Joseph recognizes this wisdom well before Solomon's time. As we learn through Joseph the ways to prevent our lusts from coming to fullness of sin, we should seek God's wisdom throughout the Scriptures, including great insight by Solomon in Proverbs 5–7.

PRACTICAL ADVICE

In the advice to his son in these Proverbs, Solomon talks about two related but different boundaries: walls keeping him away from the adulteress and walls keeping him safely within the marriage haven with his wife. Let's first look at the boundaries that Solomon advises to keep his son away from an adulterer.

> Now then, my sons, listen to me
> And do not depart from the words of my mouth.
> Keep your way far from her
> And do not go near the door of her house,
> Or you will give your vigor to others
> And your years to the cruel one;
> And strangers will be filled with your strength

And your hard-earned goods will go to the house of an alien;
And you groan at your final end,
When your flesh and your body are consumed;
And you say, "How I have hated instruction!
And my heart spurned reproof!" (Proverbs 5:7–12)

Similar to the lesson of Joseph being willing to flee, we must be willing to build boundaries to protect ourselves from lusting. We must boldly acknowledge that we can fail to the powers of lust, and we need walls to protect us from danger.

A confidant once failed to build walls when he allowed a former sexual interest to invite herself to his home to drop off something. He justified the brief interaction by saying, "I was over her. I didn't have any temptations." Later, he acknowledged the risk he took in his arrogance. To this day, he and I have an agreement that he will call or text me if a similar situation comes up. He has set boundaries to never allow himself to be in a compromising place with her, and I help him stay accountable to this promise.

Solomon's instructions require boundaries. These boundaries have to be defined beforehand and never compromised. You and I must know ourselves well enough to admit our weaknesses and identify our triggers. We know that the enemy has traps and snares with the intent to steal, kill, and destroy.

One of my boundaries is based on what I call the *When Harry Met Sally* rule: men and women cannot be close friends. It's illustrated by the romantic comedy that my wife and I often quote, and it runs counterculture to the popular belief that those of opposite genders can be the best of friends. I believe it's dangerous for a person in a committed relationship to have a friendship with someone of the opposite sex that includes detailed life conversations, one-on-one communications, and regular, isolated social engagements. In almost every situation that looks like this, one or both of the friends have a romantic interest, whether consciously or subconsciously. And in a moment of weakness, lust can overcome the best intentions between friends. I no longer fool myself by allowing these types of friendships.

To help us set and maintain our boundaries, it's crucial to have an accountability partner who is trustworthy to hear our struggles and sinful admissions—free of condemnation but able to give hard-hitting truth when we need it. He or she should know you well enough to point out your blind spots. It'll probably not be your spouse but a faithful friend, a deacon from church, or a local family member. Additionally, it's helpful to surround ourselves in fellowship with other Christians in environments of faithful accountability. Many people are more likely to fall into lustful temptations when they socialize with secular friends—who may or may not hold to a standard of righteousness—than with a group of friends with a common faith.

TWO BROTHERS, DIFFERENT OUTCOMES

Joseph is an extraordinary contrast to Judah. Joseph doesn't play the victim in his slavery. Instead, he serves Potiphar well through God's grace and is a blessing to Potiphar's entire household. With God's wisdom, he avoids the immoral wife of Potiphar. He fears sinning against God and remains steadfast against repeated temptations.

Judah, on the other hand, has a household of wickedness, plays the victim in the loss of his wife, and succumbs to the temptation of a woman he assumes is a veiled prostitute. He fails to avoid women who don't share in his allegiance to God. In foolishness, he lacks integrity and honor and acts without discernment. And in his harsh judgment, he proves to be a hypocrite.

Let us seek to learn from the mistakes of Judah and pattern ourselves after Joseph.

INSTRUCTION FOR SPOUSES

In addition to the lessons from Judah and Joseph, the Bible provides explicit instruction on sex and lust for spouses. Hebrews 13:4 says, "Marriage is to be held in honor among all, and the marriage bed is to be undefiled; for fornicators and adulterers God will judge." There are numerous commands in Leviticus 18 on whom you cannot have sex with. The Bible is clear that sex with someone other than your spouse defiles marriage.

However, nothing is said about what is allowed within marriage. Sex within marriage comes with much freedom. A study of Song of Solomon reveals some racy instructions. It's inferred that how spouses have sex is determined by each married couple.

The main thing to consider regarding married sex is to be subject to one another, to love one another. In 1 Corinthians 7, Paul says that we no longer have authority over our own bodies; we are one flesh with our spouses and need to think as such. There should be no shame in sex, so if one feels discomfort, pain, or shame, then the partner needs to show love and understanding.

In the freedom of the marriage bed, Paul says that one rule is placed upon the husband and wife: neither should feel deprived. The husband is to fulfill his duty to his wife, and the wife is to fulfill her duty to her husband.

> The husband must fulfill his duty to his wife, and likewise also the wife to her husband. The wife does not have authority over her own body, but the husband does; and likewise also the husband does not have authority over his own body, but the wife does. Stop depriving one another, except by agreement for a time, so that you may devote yourselves to prayer, and come together again so that Satan will not tempt you because of your lack of self-control. (1 Corinthians 7:3–5)

When spouses are not getting their needs for intimacy met, they can easily find themselves lusting and enduring sexual temptation. It's not an excuse to commit adultery, but when a husband or wife feels deprived—sexually or otherwise—he or she becomes a target for spiritual warfare and gets tempted by Satan himself. Why would a loving spouse allow a mate to go out of the bedroom and into the world unfulfilled and susceptible to supernatural attacks against the marriage? Do you really want to send your spouse into the world vulnerable to Satan?

A spouse who feels deprived becomes a target for spiritual warfare and gets tempted by Satan himself.

Circling back to Proverbs, we find the second type of boundary espoused by Solomon: not only do we build boundaries to protect our marriages, but we also create a cocoon of safety for the marriage relationship to thrive.

> Drink water from your own cistern
> And fresh water from your own well.
> Should your springs be dispersed abroad,
> Streams of water in the streets?
> Let them be yours alone
> And not for strangers with you.
> Let your fountain be blessed,
> And rejoice in the wife of your youth.
> As a loving hind and a graceful doe,
> Let her breasts satisfy you at all times;
> Be exhilarated always with her love. (Proverbs 5:15–19)

Similar to the boundaries that keep lust for others outside of our marriages, we should build security by nurturing our desire for our spouses within our marriages. If we can shut out all the sinful energy, then we can have the freedom to enjoy sex in the place that God intends it. There is no shame inside marriage, only joy. There is not sin, only love. There is no emptiness, only sexual fulfillment. Taking our eyes off temptations outside of our marriages allows us to see better the beauty that we have been given in our marriages by a holy and loving God. He gives perfect gifts.

God's wisdom is simple: experience freedom, joy, and pleasure in the marriage bed. Know that there is no shame in sex within the marriage covenant. Take care of each other's needs. Love your spouse the way you would want to be loved.

CONFESSION FOR SINNERS

We've focused on how to prevent lust from escalating to sin. But what if you're already involved in full-grown sexual immorality? This study is not an effort to make you feel ashamed and guilt-ridden. The truth is that most people—perhaps all people except Jesus Himself—have failed in some way regarding lust and sexual immorality. We see it not only with Judah but also many others in the Bible, including a man after God's own heart, King David.

If you feel convicted of sin, don't hide or turn away from God. You are being drawn to God through confession and repentance. Martin Luther said this:

> Beware of aspiring to such purity that you will not wish to be looked upon as a sinner, or to be one. For Christ dwells only in sinners. On this account he descended from heaven, where he dwelt among the righteous, to dwell among sinners. Meditate on this love of his and you see his sweet consolation. For why was it necessary for him to die if we can obtain a good conscience by our works and afflictions? Accordingly, you will find peace only in him and only when you despair of yourself and your

own works. Besides, you will learn from him that just as he has received you, so he has made your sins his own and has made his righteousness yours.[7]

We see this play out in David's life. Although he committed adultery that led to dreadful consequences, his confession to God resulted in grace, cleansing, and renewal (Psalm 51). You may need that right now. Turn to God in the name of Jesus, and you will be made right through Him.

---

7. Martin Luther, *Luther: Letters of Spiritual Counsel,* trans. and ed. Theodore G. Tappert (British Columbia: Regent College of Publishing, 2003).

REFLECTION ON
LUSTING

Judah's Failure
Five factors contributed to Judah's path of sexual sin: incompatible faith, greed, lack of sensitivity and discernment, a victim mentality, and foolishness. Have one or more of these factors impacted your ability to prevent lust in your life?

Joseph's Success
Four factors contributed to Joseph's success in preventing lust: God's grace, diligent labor, a willingness to flee, and God's wisdom. Which of these factors can you pray for and work on to bolster a life of sexual purity?

Practical Advice
Solomon teaches us to have boundaries to prevent lusting. What boundaries, if they had existed, would have prevented you from falling to lust in the past? What new boundaries will you consider moving forward?

Two Brothers, Different Outcomes
Judah's negligence led directly to failure, and Joseph's intentionality led to his success in the area of sexual purity. What outcome are you currently working toward?

Instruction for Spouses

While God restricts sex outside of marriage, He encourages sex within marriage as a place of freedom. The Bible establishes marital sex as a vital way to express love, develop intimacy, and protect spouses against lust. What thought, belief, or experience holds you back from enjoying the freedom of sex within marriage?

Confession for Sinners

We see the consequences of lust not only in Judah's life but also in the lives of many others in the Bible, including King David. If you've failed in the areas of lust and sexual morality, have you confessed your sin and drawn close to God in repentance?

OH GOD, WHY CAN'T I STOP
Giving In to Gluttony

MY WIFE IS A beautiful and fit woman. She eats right and has adopted a clean diet with little sugar or processed foods. She wakes early to work out at the gym, cooks healthy family meals in the evenings, and shops for quality food, often organic and local. These habits were encouraged in her upbringing, and she hopes to see it fruitful for the whole family.

And then there are the occasions when her sweet tooth takes over. My wife can eat a box of Little Debbie Swiss Rolls in one sitting. She can gobble up a two-pound bag of Haribo gummi bears—leaving two in the bag so that she can claim that she didn't eat them all. Every Halloween, she sneaks into our children's candy buckets and claims a "parent tax," a levy that would make any communist blush. Even my disciplined wife is gluttonous at times.

We often understand gluttony to describe eating or drinking too much, but the word can be applied to many more things. Its meaning is not dependent on what is being consumed but on the words *too much*. Gluttony is taking a good thing to an unhealthy excess. And while I may chuckle at my wife's occasional lapses, there's nothing funny about the devastating impact that gluttony can wreak on our lives and the lives of those around us.

Some gluttonous behavior is easy to see in addictions that have obvious, external consequences. Other forms of gluttony are hidden and quite subtle, easier to deny or dismiss. Whether gluttony is obvious or hidden, many of us know we are gluttonous and cry out, "Oh God, why can't I stop?"

GOD'S GOOD GIFTS

Throughout the Bible, we see all of the good things that God has created for us. In Ecclesiastes, for example, food and drink are recognized as good. King Solomon declared them a reward for hard work and expected them to be consumed with thanksgiving.

> I know that there is nothing better for them than to rejoice and to do good in one's lifetime; moreover, that every man who eats and drinks sees good in all his labor—it is the gift of God. (Ecclesiastes 3:12–13)

Sex is introduced as another wonderful gift from God that brings offspring into the world, gives pleasure to both man and woman, and draws two people together in intimacy. In his letter to the Corinthians, Paul explained that sex is good to build up and protect marriage against temptation.

> Stop depriving one another, except by agreement for a time, so that you may devote yourselves to prayer, and come together again so that Satan will not tempt you because of your lack of self-control. (1 Corinthians 7:5)

We also see the benefits of medicines. God is a healer who proclaims the power of herbs, foods, wine, and laughter as remedies for ailments.

> By the river on its bank, on one side and on the other, will grow all kinds of trees for food.... their fruit will be for food and their leaves for healing. (Ezekiel 47:12)

These good gifts from God are part of the fabric of our lives. Perhaps that's why we often don't discern the subtle shift from healthy consumption to unhealthy excess.

Consider our professions, for instance. God gives us work as a means to provide for our families, for ourselves, and for others. He gives us work to satisfy our creative impulses and to build something with our own hands and minds. And when we labor, we are to work heartily. Regardless of the vocations we choose or that have been chosen for us, God would have us be the best we can be. Even if our employers fail to recognize us or pay us what we are worth, we should work as if it is for Jesus Himself.

> Whatever you do, do your work heartily, as for the Lord rather than for men. (Colossians 3:23)

Yet good work can be taken too far. I grew up in a home of two hardworking parents. My dad worked seven days a week. Five days a week, he woke up around 3:30 a.m. to distribute bread products to grocery stores until 6 p.m. On his two lighter days, he worked five hours to ensure that his products were well stocked and presentable on the racks. Meanwhile, my mother was a stay-at-home mom in my early childhood who worked part-time jobs to make ends meet. As I grew older, she worked full time at a fabric store and then later as an office manager.

That work ethic was burned into me. At one stage of my life, I was traveling several days a month, and when I wasn't traveling, I would work all day, taking a short break to eat with the family and help with bedtime activities before returning to the laptop until midnight. My parents and I were some of the best at work—but not the best at rest.

God knows what we need. He is clear that He expects six days of work during the week, but He also affirms the need for rest. God is so serious about rest that He commands a day of every week to recharge. He also lays out a calendar of week-long festivals and holidays that indicate opportunities to pause work for an extended period, enjoy special vacations, and reconnect with God and the family.

> Six days you are to do your work, but on the seventh day you shall cease from labor so that your ox and your donkey may rest, and the son of your female slave, as well as your stranger, may refresh themselves. (Exodus 23:12)

It's ironic that—despite a strong work ethic—we can be susceptible to taking rest to excess too. There was a time when I watched college football on Thursday night, Friday night, and then all Saturday. I stayed up late for games on the West Coast and watched pro football on Sunday and Monday. My "day" of rest stretched into thirty hours of football each week—not to mention pregame shows, highlight reels, discussions on winners and losers, and fantasy football. I'm not alone. Sports, particularly American football, garners the highest TV ratings on a regular basis. And with the advent of streaming programs and the phenomenon of binge watching, sports is not the only form of entertainment that can be taken too far. It's not unusual for some to watch an entire season of a TV program in one weekend. Our forms of entertainment are often not the rest that God had in mind for us.

Food and drink, sex, medicine, work, rest, and entertainment—all are wonderful. God's gifts were created to serve us for our good, as Jesus said about rest:

> The Sabbath was made for man, and not man for the Sabbath. (Mark 2:27)

But when we get that order wrong—when we live as if we were made for these gifts rather than the other way around—we no longer enjoy them in moderation. God must have known we'd be tempted to reverse the order because His Word instructs us to enjoy these gifts in moderation. Sex, for example, was designed for enjoyment within marriage and must be balanced with many other priorities in life. The writer of Ecclesiastes says that there is "a time to embrace and a time to shun embracing" (Ecclesiastes 3:5). When we begin to indulge in sex and other gifts at inappropriate times and spaces, we find ourselves outside of God's will.

God's Word is full of other instructions on gluttony. Proverbs cautions:

Have you found honey? Eat only what you need, that you not have it in excess and vomit it. (Proverbs 25:16)

Yet we continue to consume things in excess. In some cases, our excess is caused by forces beyond our control. Alcoholics, for example, are unable to drink in moderation because they grapple with a dreadful predisposition toward alcohol. Their problem is defined more as an addiction than gluttony.

However, a majority of people are able to consume food and drink in moderation but choose not to do so. Perhaps in capitulation to emotions like boredom or anxiety, we allow our habits to slip into gluttony. God's good gifts then become twisted by overconsumption, leading to sin that is destructive in our lives.

To be clear, the old adage "everything in moderation" isn't true. There are some things that are not good gifts from God, things that are sinful regardless of the amount. A little pornography is not good; a little heroin is not acceptable; a little hate is not permitted. This discussion on gluttony isn't about desires outside of God's will. This study is on taking a good gift from God to excess.

TOO MUCH OF A GOOD THING

Where is the line that determines when a good thing becomes excessive in our lives?

We can turn to some metrics for guidance. Americans generally agree that we've had too much to drink if our blood alcohol level measures more than 0.08 percent. And we've had too much to eat if we consume more calories than we burn in a day. According to these guidelines, an average male of 180 pounds can consume 2,200 calories a day and two drinks in one hour. He may occasionally wash down a bowl of pasta with a Frappuccino and chocolate cake, but he can remain healthy if it's not the norm.

An inward sign that we've crossed the line is a shift in our attitude. It may be imperceptible to others, but we realize in ourselves an inability or unwillingness to respect the bounds of moderation. As we need more to feel satiated, we spend more of our time and resources on our gluttonous behavior. It's a spiral that descends until, as Paul warned the Christian community in Thessalonica, we eventually become mastered by our desire.

> Don't be a slave of your desires or live like people who don't know God. (1 Thessalonians 4:5, CEV)

There are outward signs of gluttony, sometimes immediate and tangible. When people get drunk at the company party, for example, they appear unprofessional, emboldened to flirt with coworkers, say embarrassing things, or make infamous moves on the dance floor. Paul wrote in his letter to the Ephesians that drunkenness is out of line with the call of God.

> And do not get drunk with wine, for that is dissipation, but be filled with the Spirit. (Ephesians 5:18)

Some people argue that getting drunk in the safety of friends and family is acceptable, but my experience is that drunkenness can cause terrible lapses in judgments at home. We may appear unreliable to our spouses and kids. We already have a difficult time taming the tongue, and with too much alcohol, we can say things we shouldn't say in humor, anger, or sadness. In today's connected world of smartphones and social media, there is no limit to the damage that can be done. Worse, drunkenness can trigger rage and violence, creating a danger to the very people we claim to love.

Outwardly, gluttony reveals itself by subtly and incrementally breaking down our bodies and resources over time. For example, medicines are helpful, but an overdependence eventually traps people in the tyranny of addiction. Food is delicious, but too much causes weight gain, diabetes, and heart disease. One-sixth of the American economy is spent on health care, which is directly attributed to Americans' poor eating habits.

Gluttony can also take the form of the ruthless covetousness of greed. In fact, greed may be a result of many issues: not only gluttony but envy, pride, and idolatry. Money is useful, and having prosperity in Christ is desirable, but when the desire for money becomes excessive, a person may go from being a hard worker and faithful provider to a workaholic, not trusting in the provision that God promises. In greed, we may seek independence from God's blessings, wanting to do it all ourselves. Our motivations may be due to envy, coveting that which is not currently ours. And when greed is reckless, it leads to unethical and even illegal practices, disregarding the needs of others and ruining some in its wake. Regardless of the motives, this form of gluttony, greed, turns into idolatry.

> Therefore consider the members of your earthly body as dead to immorality, impurity, passion, evil desire, and greed, which amounts to idolatry. (Colossians 3:5)

Gluttony is also evident in sex. Sex is great, but too many people are wounded by disease and addictions to pornography, prostitution, and noncommittal sex partners. Sexual addiction is a combination of gluttony and lust that is never satisfied until our bodies are damaged and our resources are drained. Many have become debtors as they throw away their lives on massage parlors and strip clubs. One young man who made minimum wage told me about a time he took a pocketful of twenty-dollar bills to a "gentleman's club." (I doubt many gentlemen were there.) He was lulled by the attention of one woman into thinking she loved him, but when he ran out of money after nearly thirty lap dances, she promptly dismissed him.

It seems unfair that some sins can remain hidden while others may not. The observable consequence of repeatedly overeating can lead to obesity; meanwhile, an adult can secretly commit the more dreadful sin of child abuse. But this reality of observable and unobservable consequences of sin should serve as a reminder not to be so quick to judge. We don't know everything. We may not know all the details about a person's eating habits or medical disposition. When we judge someone for being gluttonous, we may overlook our own gluttonous ways. Remember to show gentleness and mercy, and have the humility to know that we all need help to stop doing the things we don't want to do.

Whether our sin is observable or not, God's Word warns us that gluttony leads to laziness and poverty—poverty with our time, health, resources, and relationships.

> For the heavy drinker and the glutton will come to poverty,
> And drowsiness will clothe one with rags. (Proverbs 23:21)

We may be falling into gluttony when we allow one area of our life to eclipse another, such as when rest interferes with productivity or when entertainment gets in the way of rest, especially the opportunity to worship and serve in God's house. Too much leads to less: less work done as unto the Lord, less development of important relationships, less serving of our neighbors, and less worship of God.

Too much leads to less: less work done as unto the Lord,
less development of important relationships,
less serving of our neighbors, and less worship of God.

CONSEQUENTIAL DISOBEDIENCE

While we may want to dismiss or minimize our problem of excess, our gluttony points to a deeper problem. God takes His commands and instructions so seriously that to act otherwise is considered disobedience. Hebrews tell us that an example of this disobedience is when the people of God refuse to rest from work.

> So there remains a Sabbath rest for the people of God. For the one who has entered His rest has himself also rested from his works, as God did from His. Therefore let us be diligent to enter that rest, so that no one will fall, through following the same example of disobedience. (Hebrews 4:9–11)

We see in Leviticus how gluttony and disobedience played out for the people of Israel. God had commanded His people to rest on the Sabbath day. Not only that, but He even commanded a year of rest for the land: "But in the seventh year the land is to have a year of sabbath rest, a sabbath to the Lord. Do not sow your fields or prune your vineyards" (Leviticus 25:4). This command was a tremendous test for Israel. It served multiple purposes, including allowing the land to recover from six years of harvests, providing a means for the poor to take food from the land that grew naturally on the seventh year, and assuring the people that God would provide.

However, when God's people settled into the land, they did not obey. For 490 years, God's people failed to observe the Sabbath for the land. God was merciful and patient for many years—in fact, for centuries—but He ultimately punished the nation for its failure. He set the sentence to seventy years to allow the land to have all the rest that it had missed. Jeremiah tells us the whole land was "a desolation and a horror" and that the nations served the king of Babylon for seventy years (Jeremiah 25:11).

This was about more than breaking Sabbath laws. In their prideful refusal to rest from work, the people had failed to trust God, which in turn oppressed the poor. God punished Israel because they misused the good gift of work to the point of disobedience.

God's response to the Israelites underscores the great cost of gluttony. He does not give us work to become an idol that absorbs our energy and talents. The one true God doesn't want His gifts to eclipse our relationship with Him. As Jesus said:

> "For what will it profit a man if he gains the whole world and forfeits his soul?" (Matthew 16:26)

When we are gluttonous, our behavior is in direct disobedience to God. Refusal that is rooted in fear or pride reflects a lack of trust in God's provision. Refusal due to addiction means we are grasping at one of God's gifts as an idol and an object of our worship. Refusal due to boredom or preference is choosing personal satisfaction over worshiping God and loving our families. Regardless of our reasons for gluttony, we are prioritizing our desires over God in disobedience.

When we are gluttonous, our behavior is in direct disobedience to God.

PRACTICAL OBEDIENCE

How does God help us stop our gluttonous behavior?

The countercultural truth is that freedom from gluttony begins with obedience to God's commands. Our culture today resists God's laws as an affront to individualism, but God's commands are given to us in love. His purpose is not to burden us with impossible demands; it is to protect us and benefit society. We step into freedom when we choose to trust and follow in His commandments.

THE GREATEST COMMANDMENT

Ironically, the Greatest Commandment urges anything *but* moderation. When pressed for the most important of God's laws, Jesus called for abundant, all-in love for God and others.

> [Jesus said,] "'You shall love the Lord your God with all your heart, and with all your soul, and with all your mind.' This is the great and foremost commandment. The second is like it, 'You shall love your neighbor as yourself.'" (Matthew 22:37-39)

God wants all of our love. Ultimately, how well we love God is the measure of how well we can live and love others in a way that honors Him. But the Word defines *love* as more than a feeling or idle talk.

> Love is patient, love is kind and is not jealous; love does not brag and is not arrogant, does not act unbecomingly; it does not seek its own, is not provoked, does not take into account a wrong suffered, does not rejoice in unrighteousness, but rejoices with the truth; bears all things, believes all things, hopes all things, endures all things. Love never fails. (1 Corinthians 13:4-8)

Love is expressed through action. It is patient and kind. It rejoices, protects, trusts, hopes, and perseveres. For this reason, John wrote,

"Little children, let us not love with word or with tongue, but in deed and truth" (1 John 3:18). Jesus explained that we show genuine love for God by obeying His commands.

> If anyone loves Me, he will keep My word; and My Father will love him, and We will come to him and make Our abode with him. (John 14:23)

We can turn from gluttony when we are rooted in obedience and love for God. And we can start down a new path when we implement action.

PREPARATION

Freedom from gluttony requires intentional effort beforehand. We must change our minds and our habits, and the Bible tells us that preparation is the key to standing firm in obedience and avoiding temptation.

> Put on the full armor of God, so that you will be able to stand firm against the schemes of the devil. (Ephesians 6:11)

Examining Ourselves in Prayer

Prayer is our starting point for preparing our minds and habits for obedient living. In prayer, we confess to God who we are as sinners. It's critical that we know ourselves and are honest about the areas in which we need help. God supplies us with His protective armor: the belt of truth, breastplate of righteousness, shoes of the gospel of peace, shield of faith, helmet of salvation, and sword of the Spirit (Ephesians 6:14–17).

Examining the Day Ahead

Prayer is an opportunity to examine the day ahead. We must be alert to the challenges and temptations that lie before us. We can be certain that we'll be tested and retested in our gluttony. Proverbs 27:12 promises, "A prudent person sees evil and hides himself; but the naive proceed, and pay the penalty." We are prudent when we take the time to plan for possible dangers. Those of us who overeat, for example, may prep healthy meals or prepackage healthy snacks that are ready to grab at particularly tempting times of the day.

> Be of sober spirit, be on the alert. Your adversary, the devil, prowls around like a roaring lion, seeking someone to devour. (1 Peter 5:8)

I've had to learn how to apply this discipline in my own life. I thought I had a healthy relationship with food until a few years ago when a trip to my physician revealed that even mildly gluttonous habits were ruining my health. My blood test results showed yellow and red warnings on my weight, body mass, cholesterol, triglycerides, blood pressure, and blood sugar. I realized I had to drastically alter my eating habits.

When my wife suggested that we turn to a clean diet of unrefined and unprocessed foods, I was skeptical. It was more expensive because we eliminated every cheap food from our fridge and pantry, including bread, pasta, rice, white potatoes, sugar, sweets, and chips. We replaced them with meat and eggs, vegetables, fruit, tree nuts, and high-quality oils. No pizza. No ice cream. No cheese. No cookies at the office. No cream and sugar in my coffee. No fun.

At least no fun at first. Though it was more expensive, I began to appreciate the changes. There was always a bounty of fruit on the kitchen counters and tasty meals in the oven. I looked forward to the fresh spreads on the dinner table. I learned to smoke, grill, panfry, and roast meat and vegetables. I filled up on eggs in the morning and stayed full at the office by snacking on nuts and raisins. And I was surprised to discover how easy it was to transition to black coffee. My grumpiness from sugar withdrawal gave way to more energy, clearer skin, and less weight.

When I returned to the doctor just thirty days later, my doctor and I were both shocked by the results. My bloodwork reported normal blood pressure and cholesterol levels. Triglycerides were cut in half, and blood sugar had dropped ten points. I had lost eight pounds. I was sold.

It's been years since that pivotal first month, and I'm enjoying food more than I could've imagined. I'm more fulfilled eating at home than at restaurants, and I have fun perfecting my favorite foods in the backyard smoker. We're staying out of the doctor's office, and we have the pleasure of watching our oldest daughter introduce healthy meals to her own family. Every now and then I give in to temptation and gobble down a pizza, but I am never tempted to return to my former way of living.

I thank God for renewing my mind and my life when it comes to food. But it was more than a one-time change. It takes daily, intentional time, money, and effort to remain committed to a healthy lifestyle. My wife and I help each other prepare for the temptations we face each day.

Examining the Week

Beyond daily effort, we do well when we also examine the week ahead. A practical tip for making sure our rest, entertainment, and leisure are appropriately balanced with work and the other most important things in life is to manage daily and weekly calendars. Many of us already book our schedules during the workday to juggle meetings, tasks, and deliverables. Why should this stop with the workday? Our time outside of work is even more valuable because that is time spent with our loved ones, our friends, our God, and even ourselves. If our employers always expect hard work without regular rest, we may need to consider seeking a new organization or career. A little preparation in our calendar goes a long way to balancing our most important relationships and activities without falling into gluttony in one area.

> *Our time outside of work is most valuable because it's spent with loved ones, friends, God, and ourselves.*

Examining our Fellowship

Our preparations with God also likely will lead us to reevaluate our companions. Whereas alcoholics lose time at bars with like-minded drinkers, those in recovery seek new friends to stay the course.

> Listen, my son, and be wise,
> And direct your heart in the way.
> Do not be with heavy drinkers of wine,
> Or with gluttonous eaters of meat. (Proverbs 23:19–20)

We can ask God to help us find people who draw us closer to God and help us navigate challenges. Tell your doctor about your struggle with drug abuse, or divulge to a trusted friend about your eating disorder. Join a support group to address your addiction. Check in with an accountability partner. We allow gluttony a foothold in our lives when we hide our sin in pride or shame.

TRUE FOOD AND DRINK

You may already be familiar with the story of the prodigal son in the Bible. The wasteful and reckless son is a picture of gluttony. Many wonderful sermons, studies, and books have been devoted to this amazing parable from Jesus in Luke 15.

In the story, the son demands his inheritance before his father dies so that he can live a gluttonous life. Jesus said that "he squandered his estate with loose living" (Luke 15:13).

We discover that his spending includes prostitutes, and when he runs through all of his money, he is left for dead. His father uses that exact term. His son is dead and lost.

This kind of death must be one of the worst: throwing around plenty of money to feel important and wanted—and then after it's all spent, when the lusts and gluttony can no longer be fed, everyone flees. The addictions linger in physical and emotional withdrawals, and though your spirit is dead, your body is well enough to feel the hollow emptiness. The reality sets in that all of the people who took part in the fun don't care. This is rock bottom. And if you've ever hit bottom, then you know that there's one good thing about it. You can only look up to find a loving Father who wants to save you.

Jesus went on to tell about how the son repents, returns to his father, and is greeted with amazing mercy and grace. Luke 15 is an illustration of how God rejoices when a sinner repents and a lost soul is found.

If you are gluttonous—even if you are dead and lost—you have one hope. Come home to the loving and forgiving Father. He will supply you with true food and true drink.

> Ho! Every one who thirsts, come to the waters;
> And you who have no money come, buy and eat.
> Come, buy wine and milk
> Without money and without cost.
> Why do you spend money for what is not bread,
> And your wages for what does not satisfy?
> Listen carefully to Me, and eat what is good,
> And delight yourself in abundance. (Isaiah 55:1-2)

Christ is the only source of genuine, lasting satisfaction. He quenches our inner hunger and thirst in a way that nothing and no one in this world can. In Christ, we find a way out of the darkness of addiction and excess into light and life. There awaits an abundance of love, joy, peace, patience, kindness, goodness, faithfulness, gentleness, and self-control. We can consume this fruit of Christ without stopping. He is the one thing we can have in excess.

Christ is the one thing we can have in excess.

In his earthly ministry, a crowd reminded Jesus of the time that bread that rained down from heaven on Moses and the people of Israel. When they demanded that He make bread rain down once again, Jesus explained that He is the eternal Bread of Life that has come down from heaven.

> Jesus then said to them, "Truly, truly, I say to you, it is not Moses who has given you the bread out of heaven, but it is My Father who gives you the true bread out of heaven. For the bread of God is that which comes down out of heaven, and gives life to the world." Then they said to Him, "Lord, always give us this bread." Jesus said to them, "I am the bread of life; he who comes to Me will not hunger, and he who believes in Me will never thirst." (John 6:32–35)

Jesus is worthy of our full devotion. When we fall on our knees in humility and confess our gluttony, He doesn't meet us with condemnation. Although He knows both the public and private ways in which we indulge in gluttonous behavior, Jesus offers relief in His grace and direction in His Word.

His Word provides a particular passage that I lean on for conviction and teaching on gluttony. Proverbs 31 is well known for its description of a godly woman, but before that, it speaks wisdom to people of leadership.

> It is not for kings, O Lemuel,
> It is not for kings to drink wine,

> Or for rulers to desire strong drink,
> For they will drink and forget what is decreed,
> And pervert the rights of all the afflicted. (Proverbs 31:4–5)

This passage motivates me to be extremely careful around my wife and children, my workplace, and my church. I am seen as a leader in nearly every part of my life. I have not made it a hard-and-fast rule to abstain from alcohol, but I have learned that I am susceptible to poor judgment when I've had a couple of drinks. I have said the wrong thing. I have acted foolishly. I have let my eyes wander. Therefore, I often pass on drinking at home with the kids around. I avoid nights out with coworkers when the focus is on drinking. I attend a church that doesn't promote alcohol at church functions. And when I do have a drink, I enjoy one beverage with no rush to have a second.

Whether we realize it or not, we are all leaders in some capacity. As heirs of God and coheirs with Christ, others look to us as examples of right living. If we are willing to humble ourselves before the Lord, He will lift us up and walk with us in obedience to God's will. Praise be to God, who helps us stop our gluttony!

REFLECTION ON
GIVING IN TO GLUTTONY

God's Good Gifts

We see that God gives good gifts to enjoy in moderation for the purpose of blessing and serving us in our lives. Is there an area of your life in which you or others have noticed a subtle shift beyond healthy consumption?

Too Much of a Good Thing

There are inward and outward signs that we've crossed the line into unhealthy excess. Some are immediate, like drunkenness, while others happen over time, like the breakdown of our bodies and resources. What signs have you observed in yourself in the past? What signs do you recognize today?

Consequential Disobedience

We see in the story in Hebrews that the Israelites did not trust God's command to rest. They took work too far and depleted their land and resources. How does your gluttonous behavior reveal a lack of trust in God?

Practical Obedience

Freedom from gluttony is rooted in obedience to the Greatest Commandment. Obedience requires daily and weekly preparation with God's help. What practical ways will you build preparation into your day?

True Food and Drink

The Bible reveals that Christ is the only source of genuine, lasting satisfaction. He quenches our inner hunger and thirst in a way that nothing and no one in this world can. He is the one thing we can have in excess, the true Bread of Life that comes down from heaven. In what way will you seek to consume Him more and more?

OH GOD, WHY CAN'T I STOP
Saying Things I Shouldn't

DON'T YOU HATE FOOT-IN-MOUTH moments? Those times when you instantly regret something you said?

I remember one of my foot-in-mouth moments. I was meeting a new, young couple who were excited to visit my church. I'd hoped they would start coming to my Bible study class and begin meaningful relationships with us. I wanted to make a good impression, so I asked questions to get to know them better.

"Where are you from?" I asked.

"Pasadena!" the wife proudly proclaimed.

My mind raced to the large town just southeast of Houston proper and home to many large industrial facilities. It's adjacent to the Houston Ship Channel, which makes Houston one of the largest ports in the US. Pasadena is a strong contributor to the greater Houston economy, and it has also modernized over the last couple of decades. But these successes of the town didn't come to mind. All I thought about was the persistently foul odor wafting from the refineries and chemical plants. The town is the butt of jokes because of its smell.

"Oh wow! My wife and I recently drove out to Lubbock, and there's a feedlot just east of that cattle town that makes it smell so bad—even worse than Pasadena!"

The look on the woman's face was unforgettable. She went from pride to surprise, hurt, and anger in seconds. To make matters worse, her husband said that he knew what I was talking about because he had graduated from Texas Tech, home of the Red Raiders from Lubbock. I effectively insulted both the husband and wife, and God probably felt a little insulted as well. Oh God, why can't I stop saying things that I shouldn't?

You probably have a foot-in-mouth story. It's terrible when it happens, and it can't be undone. Ugh! When careless words escape our lips, it's embarrassing to realize how hurtful, foolish, or tactless they are. And we're completely at someone's mercy to forgive our mistake.

My words, though hurtful, didn't come with malicious intent. But there are times when my words are hurtful, and I *am* being careless and malicious. Too often in the name of humor, I make a wisecrack at someone's expense. The laughter we draw can also draw pain for others, whether or not they hear the words spoken themselves.

Yet we are commanded over and over again to use our words to build up and not tear down. Paul says:

> Let no unwholesome word proceed from your mouth, but only such a word as is good for edification according to the need of the moment, so that it will give grace to those who hear. (Ephesians 4:29)

How do we go about the first part (letting no unwholesome word proceed from our mouths) so that we can accomplish the second part (edifying others)?

The Bible has an amazing amount of content regarding our speech and the various ways that we sin with our words. One of the Ten Commandments is not to bear false witness; that is, do not lie. Several proverbs teach us to be cautious with our tongues. Jesus harshly criticizes the speech of Pharisees. And the book of James devotes a whole chapter to instruction on taming the tongue. We'll learn as many of these lessons as possible, starting in James 3.

TAMING THE TONGUE

The epistle of James was written presumably by the half brother of Jesus, not one of the twelve disciples of Jesus. James was not a believer during His lifetime but became a believer after the resurrection. He was a key leader in the church, particularly ministering to the Jews in Jerusalem. The church was persecuted there, and James was martyred as recorded by multiple nonbiblical historians. His letter is practical for a new believer, providing clear and unambiguous direction on daily challenges facing the church. James 3 is well known for a fiery exhortation to "tame the tongue."

The chapter starts with a warning for teachers and the key for being "perfect."

> Let not many of you become teachers, my brethren, knowing that as such we will incur a stricter judgment. For we all stumble in many ways. If anyone does not stumble in what he says, he is a perfect man, able to bridle the whole body as well. (James 3:1–2)

James makes it clear that we stumble in many ways. A confessed sinner knows this already, and most people agree that this is a timeless principle common to all religions and beliefs. Since we all stumble in many ways, there should be few teachers. This implies that the teachers of the Word of God should stumble less often—or not at all. What a challenge! And the judgment is stricter for those teachers. I believe that the judgment is not only from God and His holy justice but also from a watching world, those seeking to point fingers at Christian duplicity.

But the second principle from this passage is the assertion that anyone who can keep from stumbling with his words is a perfect person. It's an exaggeration, but the point is that the one who tames the tongue and doesn't stumble in speech will control the rest of what he does. James goes on to give two analogies: a bit in the mouth of a horse is small but controls the direction of the horse, and a rudder on a boat is a small device that controls the direction of the boat. Like a bit or a rudder, a tongue is small but controls the direction of the whole person.

James is not hopeful, however, that a person can truly tame the tongue. He uses harsh language to describe the tongue. Not only is it like a bit or rudder that directs; it is also like a fire that destroys.

> So also the tongue is a small part of the body, and yet it boasts of great things. See how great a forest is set aflame by such a small fire! And the tongue is a fire, the very world of iniquity; the tongue is set among our members as that which defiles the entire body, and sets on fire the course of our life, and is set on fire by hell. (James 3:5–6)

This doesn't give us much confidence! "The very world of iniquity"? "Defiles the entire body"? "Set on fire by hell"? What hope do we have? James must have known the Scriptures, as Proverbs 18:21 describes the nature of the tongue as giving life but also death. James's experiences, like mine, seem to gravitate to the damage done by our words rather than the value they bring. I regret that too often my words have brought more death than life.

Yet if we control the tongue, then we control our bodies. It's an outcome God wants, which is why He provides so much wisdom on this topic. Therefore, it's critical that we learn to control our tongues.

Jesus makes it clear that our words matter. In fact, our words indicate our true nature and will be judged by God. Observe Jesus's condemnation against the Pharisees in Matthew 12.

> You brood of vipers, how can you, being evil, speak what is good? For the mouth speaks out of that which fills the heart. The good man brings out of his good treasure what is good; and the evil man brings out of his evil treasure what is evil. But I tell you that every careless word that people speak, they shall give an

accounting for it in the day of judgment. For by your words you will be justified, and by your words you will be condemned. (Matthew 12:34-37)

This is truly convicting. We'll have to give an account on the day of judgment for every word spoken. Who can stand innocent in light of this? Only through the cleansing of Jesus's blood can I come before God in the day of judgment and have any hope in leniency. Because our words have such severe consequences, we must seek the Lord and apply His Word so that we will stop sinning.

In today's connected world, these lessons apply not only to the spoken word but also to the written word. With quick access to email, instant messaging, and social media, our written words can be even more damaging—and recorded for all to see forever. Not only are we seeking to tame the tongue, but we also need to tame the thumbs!

Seek to tame the tongue and thumbs.

THINKING BEFORE SPEAKING

The first step in taming the tongue is to learn to stop talking. James says in 1:19, "Be slow to anger, slow to speak, quick to listen." This is such practical advice, and if we're serious about it, we will change our habits. Solomon says in Proverbs 17:28, "Even a fool is thought wise if he keeps silent, and discerning if he holds his tongue." Here's the simple lesson: think first before you speak. We must learn to stop, listen, and close our mouths.

My dad had a similar rule in our household growing up: if you don't have anything good to say, then say nothing at all. Easier said than done. Have you ever wanted to lash out in anger when someone accused you or hurt you? And when doing so, did it simply escalate?

Anger is definitely a trigger for saying foolish or hurtful words. My dad's rule would ground me in silence often, as I'd want to emote in anger or crudeness in so many situations. It reminds me of one of my favorite sayings, Proverbs 10:19: "When there are many words, transgression is unavoidable, but he who restrains his lips is wise." I can be a foolish person, but I can also be wise simply by holding my tongue. Think first, then maybe speak.

It can be challenging to implement, particularly in our marriages. One time when my wife and I were in an argument, we found ourselves at an impasse. I was very angry, and because my understanding was to be slow to speak, I shut my mouth. I didn't want to say anything that I'd regret. At the same time, my wife wanted to ensure that we didn't let the sun go down on our anger (Ephesians 4:26). She wanted to talk it out to get to the source of the issue as quickly as possible. In the moment, it seemed like we were escalating the fight, but we both had good intentions and were both leaning on biblical wisdom.

We learned from one another. We agreed that night how to forever handle a situation like this one. When we're in conflict, we listen to the complaints. If I'm angry, then I clearly explain my concern that I may regret my words if we talk too soon, and I suggest a time when we can come back together and talk. It might be just ten minutes, or it might be a few days, but it's always a promise to come back together soon and discuss. In the meantime, I love her through touch to show that we are secure in our love and marriage.

Most of us can recognize when we are angry. But less obvious is sinning with hasty words when we're playful. A sharp wit is often considered a virtue that is delivered quickly and spontaneously in conversation. In the play *Hamlet*, William Shakespeare wrote, "Brevity is the soul of wit." It is my experience, however, that humorous, sharp wit gets a good laugh at someone's expense. Wit can tear down and destroy the soul.

I've recognized it in conversations with a good friend of mine. He has a physical limitation that receives much good-natured teasing from his friends. Everyone gets a laugh, except sometimes someone takes it too far. One time, I overstepped the line. I noticed a look of hurt on his face, and it occurred to me that his acceptance of the wit and jokes is his way of getting along and hiding an insecurity. When I asked him about it in private, the truth was revealed. The comments are unwelcome, and sometimes his feelings are hurt even though he knows there is no malice behind them. I realized that we liked saying hurtful things and getting a good laugh as long as we thought he could take it.

My friends and I failed in a basic instruction from Paul in Ephesians: use our words to build up and not tear down. Proverbs 12:18 says, "Reckless words pierce like a sword, but the tongue of the wise brings healing." I want to be as humorous as those comedians who ruthlessly roast people, but I'm convicted that my reckless words are like weapons. Knowing that God will judge all of these foolish, hasty comments, I'm mindful to start thinking first before speaking. If we want to stop saying hurtful things, we have to use our minds before our tongues.

We also need to be gentle in our speech. The apostle Paul compares gentle speech to that of a loving mother caring for her children.

> For we never came with flattering speech, as you know, nor with a pretext for greed—God is witness—nor did we seek glory from men, either from you or from others, even though as apostles of Christ we might have asserted our authority. But we proved to be gentle among you, as a nursing mother tenderly cares for her own children. (1 Thessalonians 2:5-7)

Many of our conversations are charged up and, if handled poorly, have consequences. Maintaining a gentle spirit in crucial conversations can disarm potential adversaries and create opportunities for effective communication. As Proverbs 15:1 says, "A gentle answer turns away wrath, but a harsh word stirs up anger." May we choose gentle words instead of harsh, angry, rash speech.

SPEAKING TRUTH OVER LYING

One of the more obvious ways we are to tame our tongues is in the Ten Commandments: do not bear false witness. In other words, tell the truth. Don't lie.

I remember my first experience with lying. When I was about five years old, all the kids on the block were hanging out in the backyard of a neighbor's house. The yard was in shambles while under construction for a pool. There were piles of dirt, equipment, and materials everywhere. My brother was one of the older kids, and somehow, we had matches. My brother taught me how to strike a match, and before long, we were creating little fires. Just at this time, a car was coming down the street, and we all ducked and hid, although I didn't know why. When I recognized the car as my mother's, I jumped up and waved! I was dragged to the ground, and we all waited a few minutes until the coast was clear. Then the fires resumed. Within minutes, one flame got too big and caught some of the materials on fire. There was a brief emergency, and my brother extinguished the flame with the nearby water hose.

On the way home, my brother instructed me to say nothing of the matches or the fire. Again, I didn't understand why. When asked by my mom what we were doing in the neighbor's yard, I froze. My brother jumped in with some explanation, but my mom didn't take her eyes off mine. When she asked for me again to explain myself, I lied. I don't remember what I said, but she knew immediately that I was lying. Before too long, there were dual spankings and groundings. It became clear to me: do not lie.

If I had told the truth, I could have explained that I didn't know or understand the prohibition against playing with matches. My loving mother would have been merciful because I honestly didn't realize we were doing anything wrong. But when I capitulated to lying, I knew I was doing something wrong. My lying was a result of me acting out in sin first. My mom was hurt that day. Not only did her sons disobey prohibitions on playing with fire, but they both lied about it. Lies cause collateral damage along the way.

Proverbs 26:28 says, "A lying tongue hates those it hurts, and a flattering mouth works ruin." This proverb proves that the tongue—which lies, hates, and hurts—is worthy of the fate laid out by James: the tongue is set on fire in hell (James 3:6). God doesn't like it. In fact, if God hates anything, it is a lying tongue and a false witness.

> There are six things the Lord hates,
> Yes, seven that are detestable to him:
> Haughty eyes, a lying tongue,
> And hands that shed innocent blood,
> A heart that devises wicked schemes,
> Feet that run rapidly to evil,
> A false witness who utters lies,
> And one who spreads strife among brothers.
> (Proverbs 6:16-19)

We all come to understand this by the time we're in elementary school, but the temptation to lie follows us into adulthood. The motive behind our natural desire to lie is often to preserve ourselves: our wealth, reputation, or desires. Lies are a secondary sin; usually the first sin is worse. When people lie on their tax returns or travel expense reports, thinking that these "little white lies" simply keep a few extra dollars in their pockets, their lying stems from stealing. When people lie about being late to a meeting because of traffic to cover the fact that they didn't make the meeting a priority, the white lie is an attempt to protect their character; their lying is the result of pride. When people lie to their spouses about whom they had lunch with at work, their white lies are hiding impure motives; their lying may be the result of lust.

Sometimes lies are motivated by a desire to punish an enemy. Jesus's accusers set up an illegal, corrupt trial to put Him to death, seeking false testimony. They hated Jesus, and they broke many of the Ten Commandments to be rid of him. Lying can be the result of hate.

God hates lying, and Jesus calls out lying and all forms of sinful speech as proof of the iniquity inside a person's heart (Matthew 12:34). If we're going to tame the tongue and stop lying, we have to address the root causes. We must first stop boasting, stop stealing, stop lusting, and stop hating, and then we'll have a chance to stop lying. We must address our hearts, and then the overflow of our hearts will be righteous speech.

We can stop lying if we first stop other sins.

BLESSING INSTEAD OF CURSING AND GOSSIPING

Another reason our tongues need taming is the duplicity in our speech. This convicting and true statement is declared in James.

> With it we bless our Lord and Father, and with it we curse men, who have been made in the likeness of God; from the same mouth come both blessing and cursing. My brethren, these things ought not to be this way. (James 3:9–10)

James goes on to state that fresh water and salt water cannot come from the same spring. And olives and figs cannot come from the same tree. In the same way, blessings and curses should not come from the same person in the body of Christ. Yet it happens—and not rarely.

It's one thing to observe the good and bad in a person, an organization, a church, or anything else. There is room for criticism and feedback. My wife and I are both teachers at our church, and we regularly ask for honest input from each other. Most people are too nice to give any critical feedback. But in love and true interest in helping one another, my wife and I are able to give constructive comments on our lessons, our style, and our preparation. We have a habit of asking about the best part of the lesson first. This allows an opportunity for praise and positivity. Then we invite critique, something to improve. And when done with gentleness and honesty, it is effective.

The duplicity to which James refers is sinister. It looks like a person who sings praises to God and prays for blessings but then in the same afternoon speaks harshly to a child, attacks the character of a friend from church, or wishes death on the referee who just cost the "good guys" the game. I know I've been that person. I'm the first to admit that I can be singing joyfully along to the praise song on the radio and then question the intelligence—that's putting it mildly—of the driver of the car in front of me.

Cursing can also take the form of harsh and ill-advised reprimands directed at our children. We underestimate the power of our speech on impressionable sons or daughters. I have lasting memories of painful words from teachers, parents, and bosses, all of which were careless statements motivated by anger, wit, insecurities, or cruelty. You can probably recall painful moments in your childhood caused by only words too. The old rhyme "sticks and stones will break my bones, but words will never hurt me" is a lie. Take a moment to remember your own pain, and be careful not to abuse the power you wield.

Also sinister is gossiping, a major problem in the body of Christ. It's defined in a few ways. The dictionary says a gossip is a person who habitually reveals personal or sensational facts about others. The Bible describes it as bad-mouthing someone with the intention to destroy the reputation of a person, regardless of whether the words spoken are true or not, and sometimes calls it slanderous speech or malicious talking. Regardless of how it is defined or referred to, most of us know what it is when we hear it. We're either excited about hearing something juicy at another's expense, or we are soured by hearing defaming and damaging personal information.

It is incompatible with God to speak as a saint to Him and to others but then to gossip as a devil to those in the community. When I say devil, I'm not exaggerating. In 1 Timothy 3:11, Paul uses the Greek word for gossips, *diabolos*, which is rooted in the same word for devil, to warn of deacons' wives being gossips: "Women must likewise be dignified, not malicious gossips, but temperate, faithful in all things." When we gossip, we are taking on the character of the Evil One.

It is incompatible with God to speak as a saint to Him and to others but then to gossip as a devil to those in the community.

If we want to tame the tongue, then we must stop speaking ill of others. As we discussed in another chapter, reserving judgment helps tremendously when tempted to assassinate the characters of others. Personally, I need to improve more in this area. A practical strategy that helps prevent me from saying things I shouldn't is to imagine that the person I'm talking about is standing right behind me.

I failed to apply this strategy at work one time. I was on the phone with a colleague, and the conversation turned toward our mutual disdain for another employee. When I made some judgmental and witty comments to get a laugh, my counterpart was silent. The next day, he explained that the other employee had just entered his office and could tell that the conversation was about him! I felt like a fool. I had cursed a man made in the image of God who didn't deserve my veiled attacks. I was wrong, and I had failed God and myself. Oh God, help me stop saying the things I shouldn't.

BUILDING UP AND NOT TEARING DOWN

Let's return to the key verse from Paul in his letter to the church in Ephesus. Ephesians 4:29 says, "Do not let any unwholesome talk come out of your mouths, but only what is helpful for building others up according to their needs, that it may benefit those who listen." We've been focusing on the front part of this verse, controlling the tongue to prevent unwholesome talk from our mouths. We're good if we just keep silent, but we're better if we exercise the second part of the verse, helping from the overflow of our hearts and building up others according to their needs.

The people around us need edification. Our spouses need words of affirmation. Our children need to hear that they are loved. Our coworkers need to hear that they are competent. Our bosses need to hear that they have good leadership qualities. Our fellow brothers and sisters in Christ need to hear that we support them and pray for them. Our parents need to hear that we honor them. Even God appreciates hearing praises to Him. As we stop sinning with our tongues, let's start doing the more useful thing of edifying and praising.

Taming the tongue is about more than not saying destructive things. It's also about saying more useful things to build up others.

If we study Proverbs and apply the wisdom of Solomon and others, we can achieve a master's degree in fear of the Lord and, among other good things, taming the tongue. Proverbs 16:24 says, "Pleasant words are a honeycomb, sweet to the soul and healing to the bones." Today and every day, use your tongue to speak pleasant words, and watch how your own heart will be healed along with the healing of others.

REFLECTION ON
SAYING THINGS I SHOULDN'T

Taming the Tongue
James compares the tongue to a rudder of a boat, steering the direction of the body. He also compares it to a great fire that can destroy, and he says that we will be held accountable to God for our words. Do your words tend to bring life or death?

Thinking Before Speaking
James encourages us to be slow to speak. Have you recently noticed a time when it served you well to withhold your words?

Speaking Truth Over Lying
Proverbs tells us that God hates a lying tongue. Often motivated by self-preservation or hate, lying is a secondary sin that covers another, worse sin. In what ways have you lied to preserve your wealth, your reputation, or your desires?

Blessing Instead of Cursing or Gossiping
Paul calls us to be dignified, not malicious gossips. How can we discern when a conversation about another person that is for a dignified purpose, such as solving a problem, descends into undignified gossip?

Building Up Instead of Tearing Down
Ephesians 4:29 instructs us to build up others according to their needs. Who would benefit from your edifying words?

OH GOD, WHY CAN'T I STOP
Being Prideful

Do you enjoy taking fun quizzes, tests, and surveys like I do? I remember one personality test that claimed to be able to determine which of the *Peanuts* characters I was most like. It concluded that I was the gullible and downtrodden Charlie Brown! Why couldn't I be Snoopy? I comforted myself with the knowledge that at least Charlie Brown is always able to keep a spirit of hope despite his gloomy personality.

But another personality test was so spot-on that it wasn't entertaining at all. It was terribly convicting. It promised to determine which of the seven deadly sins was my biggest challenge, my proverbial Achilles' heel. I was a new believer in Christ at the time, and after answering about twenty-five questions about my life and biggest temptations, I received an analysis of my results.

The report started out with praise. It said, "Based on your answers, you are certainly less tempted than most people."

Wow! I was immediately puffed up and thought to myself, "Yes, being a humble believer in Jesus, I am more righteous than most people I know."

The report continued, "But you have a major problem with pride. You think of yourself better than others."

Ouch. Painfully true. My thoughts had immediately compared myself to other people. And I had the gall to think that I was more righteous than others, which by definition is a sin of pride. One cannot be righteous and be prideful at the same time.

Most of us are guilty of the sin of pride. In *Mere Christianity*, C. S. Lewis considers pride "The Great Sin" and states rightly that no one in the world is free of this vice. He calls it "the complete anti-God state of mind."[8] And as I discovered myself, Lewis observes that pride is always manifested as being competitive: richer, prettier, smarter, more powerful, or more righteous than someone else.

Jesus has a very strong opinion about pride. In his final days, Jesus boldly spoke against the scribes and the Pharisees, even publicly and to their faces. While in the temple, Mark records the following:

> In His teaching He was saying: "Beware of the scribes who like to walk around in long robes, and like respectful greetings in the market places, and chief seats in the synagogues and places of honor at banquets, who devour widows' houses, and for appearance's sake offer long prayers; these will receive greater condemnation." (Mark 12:38–40)

Those with pride and false humility will receive greater condemnation. We see confirmation of this in Matthew 23 when Jesus harshly criticizes the scribes and Pharisees and delivers seven "woes" to condemn them.

You may not have noticed your own pride. You may not have been thinking, "Oh God, why can't I stop being prideful?" But if we're honest with ourselves, we'll likely find that we are in desperate need to correct this sin in our lives. As we'll learn in this study, pride is the sin of the devil. It was Satan who thought so highly of himself that he exalted himself above God. So when

---

8. Lewis, C. S., "The Great Sin," in *Mere Christianity* (New York: HarperCollins Publishers, 2001), 121-128.

we commit pride, we are more like the devil than we are of Christ. Oh, God, help us.

Let's learn the ways in which pride is manifested by looking at the failures of several people in the Bible who struggled with pride.

MY POWER

One way that pride is manifested is in power, as illustrated by Nebuchadnezzar, the ruthless king of Babylon during its greatest height of global dominance. Nebuchadnezzar destroyed Jerusalem and the temple of God and killed many Jews by the sword. He exiled many of God's people in Babylon, especially the best and the brightest, leaving the "undesirables" back in the devastated land. Though we may think badly of Nebuchadnezzar, the reality is he was a servant of God to do His will to bring justice on His people and the land (Jeremiah 25:9, 27:6, 43:10).

Not only was he the servant of God, but he also authored one chapter of the Bible! This is a little-known fact, but it's clear that he wrote or dictated a letter to the whole world in Daniel 4. In it, Nebuchadnezzar documented how he was struck down in his pride and hit rock bottom before being restored back to the throne.

Daniel 4 opens with a description of a dream that alarms Nebuchadnezzar. In his dream, a large tree flourishes until it reaches the highest of heights, and then a "holy one" comes down from heaven and declares that the tree be chopped down to leave only a stump. Daniel, a young man known for his righteousness, provides an interpretation. He reverently informs Nebuchadnezzar that the vision applies to the prosperous king of Babylon. Nebuchadnezzar would not only lose his grip on his kingdom but also lose his mind and live like an animal for seven periods of time until he recognizes the sovereignty of the Most High God.

Twelve months pass, and I imagine that Nebuchadnezzar has forgotten the warning from the dream. He sees the breadth of his kingdom from the roof of his royal palace and says, "Is this not Babylon the great, which I myself have built as a royal residence by the might of my power and for the glory of my majesty?" (Daniel 4:30). Too many *my* statements—*myself*, *my* power, *my* majesty. Nebuchadnezzar is blinded by his own pride. Not only does he forget the warning from Daniel, but he also doesn't attribute his power, his kingdom, or his might to the Most High God. It's even more shameful considering that Nebuchadnezzar became fully aware of God's sovereignty in the first three chapters of Daniel; it is clear who God is and that He reigns over Nebuchadnezzar.

As Daniel warned one year earlier, Nebuchadnezzar is immediately humbled. The prideful words are still lingering in his mouth when God strikes him with insanity and declares, "Sovereignty has been removed from you." As prophesied, the king endures seven periods of separation from his kingdom, his people, and his own humanity before coming to his senses.

> But at the end of that period, I, Nebuchadnezzar, raised my eyes toward heaven; and my reason returned to me, and I blessed the Most High and praised and honored Him who lives forever;
> For His dominion is an everlasting dominion,
> And His kingdom endures from generation to generation.
> All the inhabitants of the earth are accounted as nothing,
> But He does according to His will in the host of heaven
> And among the inhabitants of earth;
> And no one can ward off His hand
> Or say to Him, "What have You done?" (Daniel 4:34–35)

Nebuchadnezzar is fortunate to be restored to reason and to power. And with this blessing, he finally learns to give God the glory and recognize that his own power and accomplishments are fleeting compared to the Most High God's everlasting dominion. He concludes his letter to the world: "Now I, Nebuchadnezzar, praise, exalt and honor the King of heaven, for all His works are true and

His ways just, and He is able to humble those who walk in pride" (Daniel 4:37).

As we see in Nebuchadnezzar's story, God opposes the proud and exalts the humble (James 4:6). So we have a choice: we can humble ourselves, or we can let God humble us. I strive to choose the former, for I know what it feels like to receive the latter.

We can humble ourselves, or we can let God humble us.

MY VANITY

Pride also takes the form of vanity, a destructive force that involves comparing our physical appearance to that of another person. Vanity manifests itself in one of two ways: either we believe we're better-looking than someone else, resulting in putting others down and having an inflated view of ourselves, or we believe we're not better looking than someone else, resulting in putting ourselves down and having low self-esteem.

It may come as a surprise to many that having a low self-esteem is rooted in the sin of pride. It's healthy to have a modest view of ourselves, to know our more attractive qualities and recognize our less-desirable attributes. But pride compares to other people, so when those views become smug thoughts of "I have better clothes than him" or deprecating thoughts of "she's prettier than me," we've moved from modest and honest self-reflection to sinful vanity.

This type of pride has a very popular result in the capitalists of the world. The same movie industry that portrays the evils of vanity drives its actors and directors to promote vanity by making sure the women are prettier and the men more distinguished. Cosmetic surgeons profit off both women and men who desire to look better than other people. Luxury items are designed to set a buyer apart—to make a customer look better or more unique than others who are "common."

Of course, it is no sin to look as good as possible. Too often, however, the desire to look good turns into efforts to look *better* than other people or even our younger selves. The Bible tells us what it means to care for our bodies in a healthy way without pride: we are to treat our bodies as the temple of the Lord. Therefore, we should eat healthy foods and exercise regularly. We should rest and sleep. We should dress modestly and within our means to look attractive to our spouses (or to potential spouses, for the single folks). Overall, our efforts to look good should honor God and avoid any excessive behavior that leads to vain comparison to others.

We can learn from the mistakes of another king—this time the vain king of Tyre. After the Babylonian conquest of the Middle East, his port city on the coast of the land of Canaan was extremely prosperous, having both mainland and island fortifications. The king was full of pride, adorned with riches and splendor, even wiser than Daniel, and perfect in beauty. Indeed, a prophecy from Ezekiel declared that the king of Tyre "had the seal of perfection, full of wisdom and perfect in beauty" (Ezekiel 28:12). It's assumed that this was a reference to the king's dominion and not just the king himself. Some scholars believe that the prophecy against the king has language that applies also to the devil himself. Regardless, God saw the vanity of this king who thought much of himself. The prophecy against him says:

> "Because your heart is lifted up
> And you have said, 'I am a god,
> I sit in the seat of gods
> In the heart of the seas';
> Yet you are a man and not God,
> Although you make your heart like the heart of God. . . .
> Will you still say, 'I am a god,'
> In the presence of your slayer,

Though you are a man and not God,
In the hands of those who wound you?
You will die the death of the uncircumcised
By the hand of strangers,
For I have spoken!" declares the Lord God. (Ezekiel 28:2, 9–10)

Tyre was a very successful city for centuries, but pride comes before the fall. After Ezekiel's prophecy, the city became routinely attacked. Nebuchadnezzar took the mainland, other nations battled against the city for many years, and then Alexander the Great ultimately took the island city in an unprecedented strategy: he filled the sea with rocks and debris to create a land bridge. The Grecian army laid siege to a city once thought impossible to defeat.

Through the king of Tyre, we learn again that God opposes the proud and exalts the humble. We have no chance to succeed if God opposes our vanity.

MY INDEPENDENCE

Pride can take the form of independence, and there are perhaps no better examples of independence than in the lives of kings. In the law of Moses, before Israel had a king or expected to have a king, a few statutes were established that would apply to future kings. One was a simple command not to accumulate many horses for himself (Deuteronomy 17:16). This basically meant that the king should not rely on military might and compare his own might to that of the other nations around him; rather, he should trust in the strength of God. This was a terribly difficult command for kings to follow, including David.

Even as a man after God's own heart, King David was far from perfect. We know this because many stories about him are documented in the Bible, arguably more than anyone else except Jesus and Moses. Some stories are helpful to imitate his good behavior, some to avoid his errors. We can learn from one such error related to pride that David made late in his reign.

When his eyesight started to wane, David declared a census of his army. His motive was debatable as he seemed angry with the people of God; at the time, they were incurring God's wrath. Nonetheless, David was warned against doing this thing by his faithful commander, Joab, who challenged David against seeking delight in the size of his army. David clearly was breaking a statute of God, and God would swiftly respond.

After receiving the results of the census—an impressive 1.3 million fighting men—David realized his error. He even admitted that he had sinned greatly. It's possible David was comparing himself to other kingdoms now that he was secure in the land and experiencing relative peace. It's possible he was acting like Nebuchadnezzar and the king of Tyre, thinking that his success was of his own making. While his motive is not clear, what is certain is that David's great sin was pride. In this case, he was prideful of his own might, measured independently of God.

David and the nation of Israel suffered for David's failure and lack of leadership. God gave him a choice of how to be punished, and David chose the punishment that impacted himself the least but the people the most. He didn't want to choose a punishment that would reflect negatively on his military might (three months of defeats from the enemy) or his economic wealth (seven years of famine). He chose three days of disease, directly the wrath of God. David's logic was that he'd rather fall upon the hand of the Lord rather than men, but this choice led to the death of 70,000 people. David then had to recognize and repent of this new failure of pride. Sin begets more sin.

David's story is convicting for us today. God opposes us when we pridefully put too much trust in ourselves. For example, it was pride when my two-year-old resisted help and demanded, "I'll do it myself!" before being able to handle a task. It is pride when I calculate my net worth to see if I can provide for my family independently of God. It is pride when a business leader takes arrogant risks that backfire and cause massive layoffs. It's our pride talking when we seek such independence, to trust in our wealth, our spouses, our heritages, our knowledge, or whatever else that gets in the way of us putting our hope, trust, and confidence in the almighty God.

God opposes us when we pridefully put too much trust in ourselves.

MY HOLINESS

Another type of pride is manifested specifically in believers: comparing ourselves as closer to God than other people and, therefore, somehow better than others. Again, we can look to kings in the Old Testament as examples. There were not many good kings in the Old Testament, and even the good ones struggled with pride, as we see in the stories of two kings, Uzziah and Hezekiah.

Uzziah was a powerful and successful king. He took the throne at sixteen years old and reigned fifty-two years. And he did what was right in the eyes of the Lord, a phrase we see applied to only eight kings of the divided kingdom. And as long as he sought the Lord, God gave him success (2 Chronicles 26:5). His military might and victories earned him several accolades. But his pride got the better of him: Uzziah thought himself holy enough to be a priest of God. He entered the temple to burn incense even though he was not authorized. The true priests of the tribe of Levi attempted to stop him to no avail. His inward self-righteousness led to outward punishment: God intervened and struck Uzziah with incurable leprosy, a perpetual sign of his impurity to God.

Hezekiah also did what was right in the eyes of the Lord. He was a king who prayed reverent and beseeching prayers, which is amazing in itself as there are very few recorded instances of prayers from the kings of the Old Testament other than David (2 Kings 18–20).

Even more amazing are the responses that are recorded to his desperate prayers: in one story, the Lord defeated 185,000 Assyrians; in another, Hezekiah was miraculously healed and given a heavenly sign. Hezekiah's reign would have presided over hopeless times if God had not answered his prayers.

You'd think that a man with such a successful prayer life would avoid the snares of pride, but like Uzziah, Hezekiah also began to consider himself holy. He became puffed up after he received a miraculous sign that required the sun to retreat during part of the day so that shadows would be cast in the opposite direction (2 Kings 20:8–11). Instead of attributing the miracle to a mighty and merciful God, Hezekiah becomes prideful.

> In those days Hezekiah became mortally ill; and he prayed to the Lord, and the Lord spoke to him and gave him a sign. But Hezekiah gave no return for the benefit he received, because his heart was proud; therefore, wrath came on him and on Judah and Jerusalem. (2 Chronicles 32:24–25)

Many believers claim that God answers their prayers and speaks to them in miraculous ways. Other believers have no such experiences, which can sometimes leave them doubtful of their own connections to God and the value of their prayers. I've seen the believers with the more miraculous experiences look down on the others as less holy. If a prayerful king like Hezekiah can bring God's wrath due to pride, then none of us are holy enough to boast about our connections to God. If we're tempted to compare our holiness to others, then let us compare ourselves to Jesus, the perfect, spotless Lamb who knew no sin, and remember that we are sinners in desperate need of a Savior.

If we're tempted to compare our holiness to others, then let us compare ourselves to Jesus.

MY KNOWLEDGE

In the book of Genesis, the pride of humankind didn't appear right away. At first, the human race got off to a good start. God created the heavens and the earth, spoke light into existence, and called it good. Then He created the sky, land, sea, and vegetation and called it good. He created the sun, moon, and stars and called it good. He created the fish, birds, and animals and called it good. Then He created man and woman and called everything very good!

Three major events followed: the Fall, the Flood, and the Dispersion. Two of the events were directly related to pride, thinking that we know as much as God and that we know enough not to need Him. These ancient stories reveal the character of the human race then, and we are no different now.

In the first major event, the Fall, Eve was tempted in the garden of Eden by the fruit of the tree of the knowledge of good and evil, which "was desirable to make one wise" (Genesis 3:6). The crafty serpent told her that she would be like God, knowing good and evil. The desire to be godlike is rooted in pride, and it has destructive consequences, as it did with Eve. When she ignored the wisdom of God and ate the fruit along with Adam, sin and death entered the world. The couple endured punishment, after which God devised a plan that would redeem all of humanity back to Him—a plan that required the shedding of innocent blood. Pride wreaked havoc on a young earth.

This pride—the I-know-it-all attitude that is prevalent in many of us—is destructive not only for ourselves but also for the people around us. I have spoken to many people, both believers and nonbelievers, who think that their problems, aspirations, and hopes can be fulfilled through their own knowledge. It amazes me when people dismiss counsel from experts because they think they know better, like stubborn patients who refuse treatment from doctors because they "know it won't work." Or struggling math students who insist that they know the best techniques for solving equations. Or managers with blind spots who ignore signs that they have repulsive management styles. We're like Eve in many ways, grasping at more knowledge so that we don't have to rely on anyone else's wisdom, looking down at people we think are ignorant.

Never mind that the earth was washed by the flood. By the time of the dispersion, this type of pride had multiplied in the generations that followed Noah. When the earth became repopulated, the people shared one language and one goal: self-ascend into the heavens. "Come, let us build for ourselves a city, and a tower whose top will reach into heaven," they said, "and let us make for ourselves a name, otherwise we will be scattered abroad over the face of the whole earth" (Genesis 11:4). They constructed an impressive building known as the Tower of Babel.

At first glance, the project seemed industrious and prosperous and looked rather innocent. There was some obvious pride in seeking to make a name for themselves, but the bigger issue was their attempt to gain that status outside the will of God. If they were obedient, these people would have willingly scattered over the earth, being fruitful and multiplying as God had commanded Noah (Genesis 9:7). They would've been seeking to ascend into the heavens through worship and relationship with God, mentally and spiritually connecting with Him. They would've been less concerned about making a name for themselves and more concerned with God's holy name. They would've been like David and asked God for deliverance: "For You are my rock and my fortress; for Your name's sake You will lead me and guide me" (Psalm 31:3).

But these people sought to ascend into heaven on their own strength, on their own knowledge, and for their own name's sake. God put a stop to their attempt by changing the languages of the people, and groups of people of the same language settled in new lands. The event explains the extraordinary diversity of languages and cultures around the earth, something that materialists—those who believe in no God and no spiritual existence—have a hard time explaining.

Humankind continues to sin in the same way as the people of Babel did so many centuries ago. We attempt to use our knowledge to ascend into heaven, even so boldly as to replace God entirely with a set of theories to explain the universe. These theories are thought to be science, but real science is defined as "the intellectual and practical activity encompassing the systematic study of the structure and behavior of the physical and natural world *through observation and experiment.*"[9] It's key to understand that real science is conducted through observation and experimentation. Most of the claims to explain the origins of the universe and life are not achieved through observation or experimentation but rather unprovable theories and concepts that weakly attempt to eliminate the need for God's existence.

This "science" is founded on a theory that they cannot prove: that God does not exist. The foundational element of all these theories to explain the universe and life is rooted in an arrogance that is fundamentally unscientific. It's understandable to start somewhere in the observable universe, but it's a leap over a canyon to assert that only the observable universe exists and that God is nonexistent. Ironically, some theories of a multiverse are now acceptable to help explain the seemingly miraculous fine-tuning of the known universe even though the theory claims that billions of other universes exist that are not observable. The brilliant scientists behind these theories are more likely to believe in the existence of a multiverse than in God. It's terribly unscientific to me to believe in a multiverse, which is impossible to observe. The belief in the multiverse requires pure faith.

This is a topic that deserves rigorous investigation that stretches beyond the scope of this study but that we all should pursue with interest, an open mind, and a desire to know God. He is truly amazing. Today's science fails to acknowledge the truly amazing creation that cannot be explained by random events over long periods of time. It

---

9. Oxford University Press, s.v. "science," accessed January 16, 2022, https://www.lexico.com/definition/science.

is impossible that the universe came into existence on its own and that life randomly appeared with no intelligent creator. Lee Strobel's *The Case for the Creator* is a nice place to start. Then pursue scientists that are experts in the field: Dr. Stephen Meyer, Dr. James Ross, Dr. William Dembski, Dr. Hugh Ross, and many others who scientifically point to intelligent design.

What *is* within the scope of this study is the recognition that we fail in many ways, including this continuous temptation to believe that humans are the epitome of intelligence, that we can eliminate God and explain everything through our knowledge of the universe. The human race is incredibly small, our knowledge is humbly limited, and our existence is rather fragile. Why do we think we can arrogantly define God's creation without consulting with His infinite wisdom?

We cannot define God's creation without consulting with His infinite wisdom.

I am guilty. I've done it before. In college, I was not in faith but held a loose belief that God was real. As I started developing relationships that I thought would be lasting, I decided to define what love was. I had a girlfriend of about three months and enjoyed the excitement and euphoria that comes with budding love, and somehow I thought that I knew all I needed to know. I was nineteen years old and hadn't formed any lasting relationship, romantic or otherwise, and yet I felt qualified as a subject matter expert on the concept of love. I had a relatively easy life with two parents who provided for me and made sacrifices for me, but at that time, I hadn't acknowledged their sacrifices. I hadn't yet developed friendships that could endure turmoil or separation. I was selfish, seeking my own gain, my own pursuits, and my own development of my knowledge and intelligence.

Looking back, I see that I didn't know what I was doing. I didn't consult with the Creator of the universe, of the human race, and of love itself. I didn't listen to my parents, who had proven their love for me for nineteen years. I didn't listen to my girlfriend's parents either. Who did I think I was? I must have thought I was God Himself. I thought I could define love and that relationship on my own terms and my own knowledge, but it was an effort in futility. I learned a lot in that relationship—mostly that I was full of pride—and the fall was hard.

God tells us we will fall when we are prideful. Adam and Eve were proud and fell. The people of Babel were proud and were dispersed. The atheist scientists are proud and are stumped by the realities of the universe and of life. And I've been proud, and I've been humbled. Again and again, in the Bible and in life, we see that God opposes the proud and exalts the humble, including in our pursuit of knowledge.

MYSELF

This study has illustrated the many ways that pride is manifested. Pride is in being more powerful. It's in declaring ourselves prettier or not prettier. Pride is in being richer and independent. It's in being holier. It's in being smarter. Are any of us innocent?

Unfortunately, when I look inward, I recognize that pride is being myself. It's in my nature, and it's in yours. It is part of the wiring that comes with being a creation that is given free will. To be humble is to suppress myself. To be prideful is to exalt myself.

This is illustrated best through the Father of Lies, the Prince of the Power of the Air, the Great Deceiver, Satan himself. Isaiah provides a glimpse of the fall of Satan, his arrogant power, beauty, holiness, and self-ascension.

How you have fallen from heaven,
O star of the morning, son of the dawn!

> You have been cut down to the earth,
> You who have weakened the nations!
> But you said in your heart,
> "I will ascend to heaven;
> I will raise my throne above the stars of God,
> And I will sit on the mount of assembly
> In the recesses of the north.
> I will ascend above the heights of the clouds;
> I will make myself like the Most High."
> Nevertheless you will be thrust down to Sheol,
> To the recesses of the pit. (Isaiah 14:12–15)

This isn't the only place in the Bible that describes the devil. We see similar language in Ezekiel 28, Luke 10, and Revelation 12. Do you notice that it sounds a lot like the king of Babylon Nebuchadnezzar, whose pride was manifested in power?

Worse, it sounds a lot like us. Sometimes we make ourselves out to be like the Most High. Sometimes we dismiss God's authority and make our own claims. God has wisdom on managing money, taming the tongue, loving the enemy, forgiving our brothers and sisters, serving our neighbors, protecting ourselves from sexual depravity, and praying to a loving God. Yet we boldly tune God out, define our own rules, and reap the consequences. And then we blame God for the issues that have fallen upon humanity. We live in a society that is addicted to debt, spews hate on social media, abdicates individual responsibilities to governments, and twists God-given sexuality.

A few years ago, in a discussion about moral issues, a colleague declared his own opinions of right and wrong and his belief in universal salvation, which is that all people will be reconciled to God. He was certainly entitled to have his opinion, but he expressed himself with such ferocity that it wasn't a debate or discussion but more of a condemnation of anyone who had a different opinion.

I asked, "On what authority do you make these declarations on morality and entry into heaven?" This stunned my friend. He didn't understand my question, so I asked it a different way. "Have you gone to heaven yourself to know the way to get there? Have you created the human race such that you know what is good and bad for all people to do or not do?" He realized that he did not have the authority to make such definitive statements. Like the devil, he was self-ascending to heaven, establishing his throne, and insisting that he knew more than God.

I have exalted myself above the Most High God. I imagine you have, too. At various times, we have collectively become too much like the devil, allowing our pride to take God's place of authority. We know that God opposes the proud and exalts the humble, so we are fortunate that God has shown patience with us. We can lean on His mercy, humble ourselves, and receive the grace of God.

At various times, we've become like the devil, allowing our pride to take God's place of authority.

HIS HUMILITY

If the devil exalted himself, then we can turn to Jesus to see what it looks like to humble ourselves. Philippians provides the most direct teaching on humility.

> Do nothing from selfishness or empty conceit, but with humility of mind regard one another as more important than yourselves; do not merely look out for your own personal interests, but also for the interests of others. Have this attitude in yourselves which was also in Christ Jesus, who, although He existed in the form of God, did not regard equality with God a thing to be grasped, but emptied Himself, taking the form of a bond-servant, and being made in the likeness of men. Being found in appearance as a

man, He humbled Himself by becoming obedient to the point of death, even death on a cross. For this reason also, God highly exalted Him, and bestowed on Him the name which is above every name, so that at the name of Jesus ever knee will bow, of those who are in heaven and on earth and under the earth, and that every tongue will confess that Jesus Christ is Lord, to the glory of God the Father. (Philippians 2:3-11)

Jesus is amazing. Even though He existed in the form of God, He did not regard equality with God a thing to be grasped. Jesus is the manifestation of God on earth, and yet he took on the body of a human, even a baby boy needing to nurse, have His diaper changed, and learn to walk. He became frail enough to hunger, thirst, and feel the excruciating pain of the cross. This is humility: to be God but live like a man. Jesus did so in submission to God; He considered the need of all humanity—that we needed a Savior—as more important than Himself. And in the end, God exalted Him.

Philippians gives us a very practical instruction in preventing pride: regard one another as more important than ourselves. What does that look like in you and in me? It looks like a husband who tends to his wife's needs before himself. It looks like a parent who empathizes with the struggles of her child. It's a leader who listens to the feedback of those around him. It's a driver who yields to another driver on the road. A wealthy person giving generously to the poor. A healthy person serving the unhealthy. A person of strong faith lifting up a person of little faith. A person humbled by sin forgiving those who have sinned against him. A believer having compassion on unbelievers.

God takes a different tone with His people when it comes to pride. He showed patience with Peter in his failure. He was gentle with Elijah in his depression. He redeemed Naomi in her bitterness. He saved Nineveh despite Jonah's hate. He even showed mercy for David's judging of others. But this study reveals that God has less patience, gentleness, redemption, and mercy for pride. He opposes the proud and exalts the humble. Let us seek to humble ourselves before our almighty God does it for us.

God takes a different tone with His people when it comes to pride.

REFLECTION ON
BEING PRIDEFUL

My Power
At the height of his power, Nebuchadnezzar admires the breadth of his kingdom and attributes all of his success to himself. He forgets the warning from Daniel and doesn't credit God for his power, his kingdom, or his might. When you're at the top of your game, do you walk in humility and credit God's good gifts? Or do you strut in pride and pat yourself on the back?

My Vanity
The Bible calls us to treat our bodies as the temple of the Lord. But healthy self-reflection on personal appearance can become corrupted by the vanity of comparing ourselves with others. Have you identified areas in which you compete with others and conclude that you're better or lower than they?

My Independence
The law of Moses commanded that kings not accumulate many horses for themselves so that they wouldn't rely on military might and compare their might to that of the other nations. It was a difficult command for kings to follow back then, and reliance on God remains difficult for some of us today. In what ways do you seek to be independent of the might of God and rely on your own strength?

My Holiness
Righteous and prayerful kings like Uzziah and Hezekiah assessed themselves as holy, and their holier-than-thou attitudes brought God's wrath. Do you think of yourself as holier than others rather than a sinner in desperate need of a Savior?

My Knowledge
From Eve in the garden of Eden to atheist scientists today, we've seen the arrogance and destructiveness of know-it-all attitudes. In what areas of your life does your pursuit of knowledge eclipse your trust in God's wisdom?

Myself
The description of the devil in the Bible sounds a lot like King Nebuchadnezzar—and us. Do you recognize a time when you self-ascended to heaven, established your throne, and insisted that you know more than God?

His Humility
Jesus modeled the instruction given in Philippians: regard one another as more important than yourselves. Whose needs have you resisted considering as more important than your own?

A Letter to the Reader

Dear Reader,
It is my joy that you've completed *Oh God, Why Can't I Stop?* Thank you for joining me in studying a series of challenges in our walks with God. Together, we've observed that He responds to us with grace, mercy, instruction, and discipline. His response conquers our shame and paves the way to our victory in Christ. I pray that you contemplate this study and wonder at our almighty Father! He can take our failures and give us second chances, often with tremendous compassion and gentleness.

My life experiences attest to the character of God. I have failed many times and in many ways throughout my faith journey, yet He is steadfast with His love. He still keeps me and uses me, and I believe the same can be true for you. All the honor, praise, and glory be to Jesus Christ, who takes away my sins!

Before I close, I want to mention three things to you.

First, please take a minute to leave a book review online. I enjoy reading positive comments as well as constructive feedback on how this study might be improved. Did a particular topic resonate with you? Did I miss a topic you struggle with—one that causes you to ask, "Oh God, why can't I stop?"

Second, I'm available for speaking engagements. It's my privilege to talk with groups, churches, and other organizations about how God responds to our failures. You can contact me online at www.stellarwriter.com/jasonritchie or by email at jason@stellarwriter.com.

Third, and most importantly, if you are not certain of your own faith journey—if you're unsure that you have saving faith in the Lord Jesus—please reach out to me or to your local evangelical church. We want nothing more than to talk with you about Jesus, the Son of God, the sacrifice for your failures, who is risen from the dead. He is so good. He loves you and gives you eternal life by God's grace through faith in Him.

Be at peace. May God bless you.

Jason Ritchie

About the Author

Jason Ritchie came to a saving knowledge of the Lord Jesus Christ in 1996. At the time, he had just landed his dream job as a NASA software engineer for the International Space Station, but he still found himself at twenty-four years old feeling lost and unfulfilled. Although he had been raised in a Christian home, he knew something deeper was missing.

When a trusted friend at work invited him to church, Jason found a community of people who shared their hope and joy in Christ. He began to learn about his Savior and came to an adult understanding of the missing piece: his purpose was not rooted in his career or efforts but in Jesus Christ alone. And with that, everything changed.

Twenty-five years later, Jason continues to grow in his faith through prayer, study, success, failure, and redemption. He is a leader and teacher in his church in Houston, Texas. He is also an executive at a financial institution, leading real estate and information technology efforts. He holds a bachelor of science in aerospace engineering from Texas A&M University and an executive MBA in commercial banking from Sam Houston State University.

Jason is married to his wife (and publisher) Ella and has four children—and one new grandchild at the time of this publication. *Oh God, Why Can't I Stop?* is his first book.

Book a speaking engagement, ask a question, or find out about his next book by visiting www.stellarwriter.com/jasonritchie or by emailing jason@stellarwriter.com.

 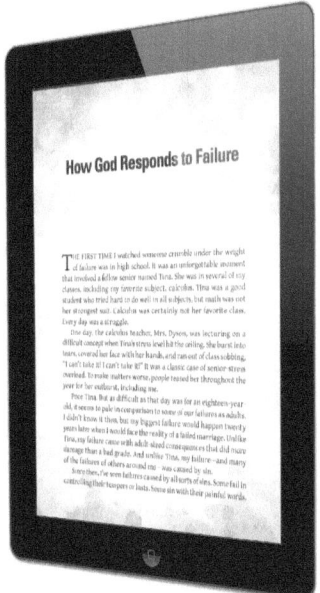

Available at your favorite online retailer in hardcover, paperback, and e-book formats.

www.ingramcontent.com/pod-product-compliance
Lightning Source LLC
Chambersburg PA
CBHW030151100526
44592CB00009B/227